GENOCIDE

GENOCIDE

RWANDA AND BURUNDI

EDWARD L. NYANKANZI

SCHENKMAN BOOKS, INC.
ROCHESTER, VERMONT

Copyright © 1998

Schenkman Books, Inc.
118 Main Street
Rochester, Vermont 05767

schenkma@sover.net

Library of Congress Cataloging-in-Publication Data

Nyankanzi, Edward L., 1943–
    Genocide: Rwanda and Burundi / by Edward L. Nyankanzi.
        p.   cm.
    Includes bibliographical references and index.
    ISBN 0-87047-105-8 (cloth)
    1. Burundi—Politics and government. 2. Rwanda—History—Civil War, 1994.
    3. Genocide—Rwanda. 4. Genocide—Burundi.
    5. Tutsi (African people)—Crimes against. I. Title.
    DT450. 85.N93 1997
    967.57104–dc21   97–773
                                        CIP

Printed in the United States of America.

To the memory of
my father Rwehera,
my mother Kadondogori,
and my children
Hope Inarukundo,
David Rwehera,
and
Ras Rwehera.

CONTENTS

ACKNOWLEDGMENTS

I am indebted to
my country,
my parents,
my teachers,
my friends,
and
the unknown.

INTRODUCTION

Genocide[1] is a special case of murder.
It is as old as mankind itself.

In 1948 the United Nations (UN) Convention on the Prevention and Punishment of the Crime of Genocide defined genocide as:

> ... any of the following acts committed with the intent to destroy, in whole or in part, a national, ethnical, racial, or religious groups, as such: a. Killing members of the group; b. Causing serious bodily or mental harm to members of the group; c. Deliberately inflicting on the group conditions of life calculated to bring about its physical destruction in whole or in part; d. Imposing measures intended to prevent births within the group; e. Forcibly transferring children of the group to another group. (Article II, *The Statutes of the United Nations Convention on the Prevention and Punishment of the Crime of Genocide.* New York: United Nations Department of Public Information DPI/1055, December 1991)

Genocide is also defined as the promotion and execution of policies by a state or its agents that result in the deaths of a substantial portion of a group. Genocide may be retributive, institutional, utilitarian, monopolistic, or ideological. In a genocidal situation the targeted group is identified as the enemy or potential enemy. The group is accused of collective guilt. The targeted group is demonized, dehumanized, and denigrated.

Related to genocide is ethnocide, the destruction of collective memory, identity, spirit, and culture without the immediate physical destruction of the targeted group. It occurs when the culture of a people is destroyed and the continued existence of a group is threatened through acculturation, detribalization, or assimilation.

1

The various methods of ethnocide include destruction of artifacts, religious icons, and traditional forms of authority, as well as relocation of ethnic groups. Ethnocide can be an alternative, prelude, or complimentary measure to genocide.

1

GENOCIDE IN
RWANDA AND BURUNDI

1

Rwanda

Landlocked in the Milles Collines, Rwanda is a fertile land where once peaceful farmers grew a variety of vegetables, cereals, and fruits, and raised their cattle, goats, and sheep. Prior to colonialism, the three ethnic groups—Abahutu, Abatutsi, and Abatwa—lived in their respective hills in a kind of symbiotic relationship. Formal institutions such as modern schools, churches, hospitals, and government institutions were nonexistent with the exception of *la Grande ecole des sciences politiques et sociales,* a school reserved for selected children of nobility.

Candidates for high offices spent their leisure time learning the art of politics, refining manners and speech, and competing in athletic activities such as high jumping, spear throwing, archery, and the art of warfare.

The class of nobility was referred to as *imfura.* The *umwami* was a remote divine personality. *Umwami* ruled through a network of *abaganwa* and *abatware.* The rest of the population were engaged in various economic activities: Abatutsi raised cattle, Abahutu farmed, and Abatwa hunted and made tools. All three ethnic groups lived side by side harmoniously. They spoke the same language and worshipped the same Imana. Ethnic consciousness was almost nonexistent.

The institution of *ubuhake*, in which individual contractors agreed on mutual obligations, was not legally binding. Social mobility was open to all. After five centuries of peaceful cohabitation it was difficult to visually recognize one ethnic group from the other. A Muhutu could be mistaken for an Umututsi and vice versa. The family lineage was based on a patrilinear system.

The Berlin Conference (1884–85), which sanctioned the partition of Africa, changed the political landscape of Rwanda. Rwanda fell under the German-East African Empire. Military expeditions led by Prussian Junkers found a well-organized kingdom similar to their own. Rwanda succumbed to German colonial rule after a short but fierce military resistance.

Belgium inherited Rwanda from Germany following the First World War. Preoccupied with the mineral-rich Congo, Belgium, like Germany, had adopted a system of indirect rule through the traditional political system. This system consisted of leadership through *umwami* and *abaganwa*. The ruling Tutsi hierarchy was transformed into paid colonial agents. The masses, both Hutu and Tutsi, were recruited into gang-like labor forces to build roads, bridges, and other public infrastructures.

Unlike his father Mwami Rwabugiri, Mwami Mutara Rudahirwa[2] was a willing partner of the Belgian colonists and Catholic Church. Rwanda was nicknamed *Urwanda rwa Bikiramariya* (Virgin Mary's Rwanda). Mwami Mutara Rudahirwa departed from colonial policy and demanded independence at the end of the 1950s.

Childless, Mwami Mutara Rudahirwa died mysteriously in 1959 in Bujumbura. Rumors suggest he was injected with poison by Belgian Dr. Julien Vyncke. Conservatives rallied around his half-brother, Prince Jean Ntahindurwa, who was crowned Mwami Kigeri V.[3]

Young Tutsi Turks rallied around *Union nationale Rwandaise* (UNAR) and demanded immediate independence from Belgium. UNAR allied itself with Patrice Lumumba's *Mouvement nationale Congolais* (MNC), Mwalimu Julius Kamparage Nyerere's Tanganyika National Union (TANU), and Louis Rwagasore's *Union et progres nationale* (UPRONA).

UNAR flirted with the Communist bloc, a political jest that irritated Belgian colonists. Belgian colonists responded by siding with *Party pour l'emancipation Hutu* (PARMEHUTU). PARMEHUTU was led by Gregoire Kayibanda,[4] then the private secretary of a Catholic bishop. Mwami Kigeri V was overthrown in 1960 and the country fell to the PARMEHUTU. That was the end of a five-century monarchy in Rwanda and the beginning of endless systematic Tutsi persecution.

Tutsi genocide began in Gikongoro in 1959. At the instigation of a local mayor, Hutu peasants armed with machetes, pickaxes, spears, bows, arrows, clubs, and even hoes, began to hunt down innocent

Tutsi men, women, and children.[5] The normal tools of survival were transformed into instruments of Tutsi massacre. Belgian authorities assisted with helicopters. This type of genocidal activity was unknown in Rwanda's culture and it was to repeat itself with regularity.

The once proud Rwandese Tutsi trekked to neighboring Burundi, Tanzania, Uganda, and the Democratic Republic of the Congo (Zaire). Like ancient Israelites, the Tutsi found themselves wandering from country to country, despised and without a permanent home. In Burundi, where their distant cousins held power, some prospered.

In Uganda, President Milton Obote expelled the Tutsi he associated with the Abanyankole.[6] Thousands were massacred in what is known as the Luwero Triangle. In the eastern Kivu Province of the Rutshuru region, Democratic Republic of the Congo (Zaire), Tutsis were massacred. In Tanzania they were often refused citizenship papers. Others were dispersed throughout Africa, Europe, and the United States. Many succeeded in their professions but continued to feel like strangers without a home.

Belgian-assisted Tutsi genocide in Rwanda and subsequent Hutu control of the country did not alleviate the Hutu's inferiority complex. Hutu leaders remained apprehensive of eventual Tutsi revenge. The Hutu-dominated government established a strict ethnic quota system in schools, businesses, and employment. Ethnic identification cards were issued and the "ten commandments"—laws which prohibited inter-ethnic sexual contact, illicit or otherwise—were published. Belgian and French co-operants continued to exercise decision-making power.

Hutu apprehension became a reality. On 1 October 1994 at 2:30 P.M., approximately four thousand Tutsi exiles under the aegis of the Rwandan Patriotic Front (RPF), also known as Inkotanyi,[7] attacked Rwanda's military positions from Kagitumba. The ill-planned invasion initially failed. The RPF suffered great losses and most of their soldiers were killed, including the commander, General Frederick Rwigyema.[8] The rest were temporarily demoralized. President Juvenal Havyarimana retaliated by arresting anyone suspected of collaborating with the RPF. Tutsis were beaten, tortured, and murdered. Tutsi homes were looted. Tutsi women were raped. It looked as if President Havyarimana's plan succeeded.

Paul Kagame[9] rushed home from Fort Leavenworth, Kansas (United States). He became the commander of the RPF and succeeded in convincing his followers that fighting was not a matter of guns or territory but a state of mind. With a sense of mission he devised new strategies. The RPF regrouped and launched a new attack from the forested Vilunga mountains. They successfully captured fertile land in the northwestern region of Byumba and Ruhengeri, the home of President Havyarimana.

Unable to contain the invading army, President Havyarimana sought military assistance from France, Belgium, and the Democratic Republic of the Congo (Zaire). France dispatched the *Deuxieme regiment etranger parachutiste*.[10] Belgium contributed paratroopers and the Democratic Republic of the Congo (Zaire) sent its *Division speciale presidentielle*. The soldiers, however, were more interested in drinking and womanizing than defending the corrupt regime of President Havyarimana. RPF forces were not scared. Instead they consolidated their position on the conquered territory.

Stalemated, President Havyarimana sought multilateral military intervention. The Organization of African Unity (OAU) proved to be ineffective. The United Nations (UN) Security Council reluctantly approved a token military contingent of twenty-five hundred peacekeepers (warkeepers) in a mandate to reinforce the Arusha Peace Accords,[11] which none of the signatories had taken seriously. UN peacekeepers patrolled the demilitarized zone and guarded buildings. On paper it looked good but *la cohabitation pacifique a la francaise* was bound to end in divorce.

The unexpected assassination of President Melchior Ndadaye and the subsequent inter-ethnic strife in Burundi became a cataclysm for Rwanda.[12] President Havyarimana abandoned the politics of reconciliation in favor of the politics of Hutization. In one broadcast by *Radio television libre des Milles Collines*, the announcer called for ethnic cleansing when he said, "The graves are half-full. Take the machetes and fill them."

Meanwhile President Havyarimana increased his military forces from five thousand to thirty thousand; bought more weapons from France, Egypt, and South Africa; and recruited and trained the paramilitary units known as Interahamwe and Impuzamigambi.

On 6 April 1994 at approximately 8 P.M., while returning from the Summit Conference in Dar-es-Salaam, President Havyarimana's French-made presidential Mystere airplane disappeared over the skies of Kigali. President Havyarimana and his colleague, President Cyprien Ntaryamira of Burundi, were later found lying next to each other on a bed of roses in the presidential garden. The Mystere's wings were found resting on banana trees and its engine in the presidential swimming pool. That was the end of Havyarimanism and the beginning of the "final solution."

Within twenty-four hours Kigali was mounted with roadblocks. The Presidential Guard moved from house to house killing opposition leaders. Among the first victims were Prime Minister Agathe Uwilingiyimana, several cabinet ministers, and ten Belgian UN peacekeepers.[13] What began as a political act turned into a campaign of Tutsi genocide. The Presidential Guard was joined by the army and the militia, Interahamwe and Impuzamigambi.

Armed with grenades, AK assault rifles, machetes, spears, knives, and nail-spiked clubs, Hutu hoodlums moved from house to house, hospital to hospital, and village to village, slaughtering every Tutsi in sight.[14] Men's genitals were cut off, women's breasts were sliced, children were impaled on sticks, babies were sliced into halves, and skulls were cracked open. Tutsi victims were buried in mass graves, thrown in nearby bushes, or left rotting in alleys, churches, classrooms, courtyards, and their own houses. Some Tutsis were buried up to their necks and left for dead. Other had their eyes gouged out. Thousands of Tutsis were rounded up, had their hands tied behind their backs, and were thrown into the Akagera River. Vultures, dogs, and wild pigs were seen feasting on the once proud Tutsi. As one priest commented, "There are no devils left in Hell. They are all in Rwanda."

The provisional government fled to Gitarama under RPF military pressure. On 13 June 1994 the provisional government fled again, this time to Gisenyi. The RPF kept the pressure on. Butare, the second largest city, fell on 6 July 1994. Kigali followed. On 16 July 1994, Gisenyi was also captured. Drunken and drugged Rwandan soldiers abandoned their weapons and sought refuge across the border in the Democratic Republic of the Congo (Zaire). A million Hutu joined the exodus. That was the end of Hutuism in Rwanda.

After four years of Tutsi massacre by the Hutu-controlled army, the RPF finally succeeded in defeating the Rwandan army through a combination of perseverance, motivation, and discipline. On 18 July 1994 General Paul Kagame, the RPF commander, unilaterally announced the cease-fire:

> We have captured all of Rwanda up to the French protection zone and a cease-fire is effectively in place. There is no need for anyone to flee Rwanda. We guarantee all Rwanda stability and security.[15]

But General Kagame's security guarantees were not convincing to Hutu refugees:

> You better escape because the Tutsi will kill you in revenge, and if you don't escape you are a traitor and we will kill you. They want to govern us from on top, like they did for a hundred years. If you go home, the Tutsi will gouge your eyes out, steal your property, and make you slaves.

Regardless of repeated assurances, the Hutu remained scared. It was widely believed that the Tutsi would kill the Hutu out of hatred and a desire to be superior. Though frightened, the Hutu were not without hope. A Hutu declared, "The war is not over. If we can get weapons, we will fight again. We will re-attack and we will win this time."

While Hutu refugees were reluctant to return to Rwanda, Tutsis were returning to occupy deserted houses, businesses, and farms. In Nyamata, now known as an historic site of Tutsi massacre, thousands of Tutsi refugees returned from Uganda to occupy abandoned fields and houses.[16] Returned Tutsi refugees opened shops and revived the economy in Gisenyi. Tutsi soldiers patrolled the streets and countryside, zig-zagging the roads in pick-up trucks. One soldier joyfully remarked, "Nous sommes chez nous" (We are home).

Appendix I

Statute of the United Nations International Tribunal for Rwanda

Having been established by the Security Council acting under Chapter VII of the Charter of the United Nations, the International Criminal Tribunal for the Prosecution of Persons Responsible for Genocide and Other Serious Violations of International Humanitarian Law Committed in the Territory of Rwanda and Rwandan citizens responsible for genocide and other such violations committed in the territory of neighboring States, between 1 January 1994 and 31 December 1994 (hereinafter referred to as "the International Tribunal for Rwanda") shall function in accordance with the provisions of the present Statute.

Article I
Competence of the International Tribunal for Rwanda

The International Tribunal for Rwanda shall have the power to prosecute persons responsible for serious violations of international humanitarian law committed in the territory of Rwanda and Rwandan citizens responsible for such violations committed in the territory of neighboring States, between 1 January 1994 and December 1994, in accordance with the provisions of the present Statute.

Article 2
Genocide

1. The International Tribunal for Rwanda shall have the power to prosecute persons committing genocide as defined in paragraph 2 of the article or of committing any of the other acts enumerated in paragraph 3 of this article.

13

2. Genocide means any of the following acts committed with intent to destroy, in whole or in part, a national, ethnical, racial or religious group, as such:

   (a) Killing members of the group;

   (b) Causing serious bodily injury or mental harm to members of the group;

   (c) Deliberately inflicting on the group conditions of life calculated to bring about its physical destruction in whole or in part;

   (d) Imposing measures intended to prevent births within the group;

   (e) Forcibly transferring children of the group to another group.

3. The following acts shall be punishable:

   (a) Genocide;

   (b) Conspiracy to commit genocide;

   (c) Direct and public incitement to commit genocide

   (d) Attempt to commit genocide;

   (d) Complicity in genocide.

Article 3
Crimes against humanity

The International Tribunal for Rwanda shall have the power to prosecute persons responsible for the following crimes when committed as of a widespread or systematic attack against any civilian population on national, political, ethnic, racial, or religious grounds:

   (a) Murder;

   (b) Extermination;

   (c) Enslavement;

   (d) Deportation;

   (e) Imprisonment;

   (f) Torture;

(g) Rape;

(h) Persecutions on political, racial and religious grounds;

(i) Other inhumane acts.

Article 4
Violations of Article 3 common to the Geneva Conventions and of Additional Protocol II

The International Tribunal for Rwanda shall have the power to prosecute persons committing or ordering to be committed serious violations of Article 3 common to the Geneva Conventions of 12 August 1949 for the Protection of War Victims, and of Additional Protocol II thereto at 8 June 1977. These violations shall include, but shall not be limited to:

(a) Violence to life, health and physical or mental well-being of persons, in particular murder as well as cruel treatment such as torture, mutilation or any form of corporal punishment;

(b) Collective punishments;

(c) Taking of hostages;

(d) Acts of terrorism;

(e) Outrages upon personal dignity, in particular humiliating and degrading treatment, rape, enforced prostitution and any form of indecent assault;

(f) Pillage;

(g) The passing of sentences and the carrying out of executions without previous judgment pronounced by a regularly constituted court, affording all the judicial guarantees which are recognized as indispensable by civilized peoples;

(h) Threats to commit any of the foregoing acts.

Article 5
Personal jurisdiction

The International Tribunal for Rwanda shall have jurisdiction over natural persons pursuant to the provisions of the present Statute.

Article 6
Individual criminal responsibility

1. A person who planned, instigated, ordered, committed or otherwise aided and abetted in the planning, preparation or execution of a crime referred to in Article 2 to 4 of the present Statute, shall be individually responsible for the crime.

2. The official position of any accused person, whether as Head of State or Government or as a responsible Government official, shall not relieve such person of criminal responsibility nor mitigate punishment.

3. The fact that any of the acts referred to in Articles 2 to 4 of the present Statute was committed by a subordinate does not relieve his or her superior of criminal responsibility if he or she knew or had reason to know that the subordinate was about to commit such acts or had done so and the superior failed to take the necessary and reasonable measures to prevent such acts or to punish the perpetrators thereof.

4. The fact that an accused person acted pursuant to an order of a Government or of a superior shall not relieve him or her of criminal responsibility, but may be considered in mitigation or punishment if the International Tribunal for Rwanda determines that justice so requires.

Article 7
Territorial and temporal jurisdiction

The territorial jurisdiction of the International Tribunal for Rwanda shall extend to the territory of Rwanda including its land surface and airspace as well as to the territory of neighboring States in respect of serious violations of international humanitarian law committed by Rwandan citizens. The temporal jurisdiction of the International Tribunal for Rwanda shall extend to a period beginning on 1 January 1994 and ending on 31 December 1994.

Article 8
Concurrent jurisdiction

1. The International Tribunal for Rwanda and national courts shall have concurrent jurisdiction to prosecute persons for serious violations of international humanitarian law committed in the territory of Rwanda and Rwandan citizens for such violations committed in the territory of neighboring States, between 1 January 1994 and 31 December 1994.

2. The International Tribunal for Rwanda shall have primacy over the national courts of all States. At any stage of the procedure, the International Tribunal for Rwanda may formally request national courts to defer to its competence in accordance with the present Statute and the Rules of Procedure and Evidence of the International Tribunal for Rwanda.

Article 9
Non bis in idem

1. No person shall be tried before a national court for acts constituting serious violations of international humanitarian law under the present Statute, for which he or she has already been tried by the International Tribunal for Rwanda.

2. A person who has been tried by a national court for acts constituting serious violations of international humanitarian law may be subsequently tried by the International Tribunal for Rwanda only if:

   (a) The act for which he or she was tried was characterized as an ordinary crime; or

   (b) The national court proceedings were not impartial or independent, were designed to shield the accused from international criminal responsibility, or the case was not diligently prosecuted.

3. In considering the penalty to be imposed on a person convicted of a crime under the present Statute, the

International Tribunal for Rwanda shall take into account the extent to which any penalty imposed by a national court on the same person for the same act has already been served.

Article 10
Organization of the International Tribunal for Rwanda

The International Tribunal for Rwanda shall consist of the following organs:

(a) The Chambers, comprising two Trial Chambers and an Appeals Chamber;

(b) The Prosecutor; and

(c) A Registry.

Article 11
Composition of the Chambers

The Chambers shall be composed of eleven independent judges, no two of whom may be nationals of the same State, who shall serve as follows:

(a) Three judges shall serve in each of the Trial Chambers;

(b) Five judges shall serve in the Appeals Chamber.

Article 12
Qualification and election of judges

1. The judges shall be persons of high moral character, impartiality and integrity who possess the qualifications required in their respective countries for appointment to the highest judicial offices. In the overall composition of the Chambers due account shall be taken of the experience of the judges in criminal law, international law, including international humanitarian law and human rights law.

2. The members of the Appeals Chamber of the International Tribunal for the Prosecution of Persons Responsible for Serious Violations of International Law Committed in the Territory of the Former Yugoslavia since 1991 (hereinafter

referred to as "the International Tribunal for the Former Yugoslavia") shall also serve as the members of the Appeals Chamber of the International Tribunal for Rwanda.

3. The judges of the Trial Chambers of the International Tribunal for Rwanda shall be elected by the General Assembly from a list submitted by the Security Council, in the following manner:

   (a) The secretary shall invite nominations for judges of the Trial Chambers from States Members of the United Nations and non-member States maintaining permanent observer missions at United Nations Headquarters;

   (b) Within thirty days of the date of the invitation of the Secretary-General, each State may nominate up to two candidates meeting the qualifications set out in paragraph 1 above, no two of whom shall be of the same nationality and neither of whom shall be of the same nationality as any judge on the Appeals Chamber;

   (c) The Secretary-General shall forward the nominations received to the Security Council. From the nominations received the Security Council shall establish a list of not less then twelve and not more than eighteen candidates, taking due account of adequate representation on the International Tribunal for Rwanda of the principal legal systems of the world;

   (d) The President of the Security Council shall transmit the list of candidates to the President of the General Assembly. From that list the General Assembly shall elect the six judges of the Trial Chambers. The candidates who receive an absolute majority of the votes of States Members of the United Nations and of the non-Member States maintaining permanent observer missions at United Nations Headquarters, shall be declared elected. Should two candidates of the same nationality obtain the required majority vote, the one who received the higher number of votes shall be considered elected.

4. In the event of a vacancy in the Trial Chambers, after consultation with the Presidents of the Security Council and of the General Assembly, the Secretary-General shall appoint a person meeting the qualifications of paragraph 1 above, for the remainder of the term of office concerned.

5. The judges of the Trial Chambers shall be elected for a term of four years. The terms and conditions of service shall be those of the judges of the International Tribunal for the Former Yugoslavia. They shall be eligible for re-election.

Article 13
Officers and members of the Chambers

1. The judges of the International Tribunal for Rwanda shall elect a President.

2. After consultation with the judges of the International Tribunal for Rwanda, the President shall assign the judges to the Trial Chambers. A judge shall serve only in the Chamber to which he or she was assigned.

3. The judges of each Trial Chamber shall elect a Presiding Judge, who shall conduct all of the proceedings of that Trial Chamber as a whole.

Article 14
Rules of procedure and evidence

The judges of the International Tribunal for Rwanda shall adopt, for the purpose of proceedings before the International Tribunal for Rwanda, the rules of procedure and evidence for the conduct of the pre-trial phase of the proceedings, trials and appeals, the admission of evidence, the protection of victims and witnesses and other appropriate matters of the International Tribunal for the Former Yugoslavia with such changes as they deem necessary.

Article 15
The Prosecutor

1. The Prosecutor shall be responsible for the investigation and prosecution of persons responsible for serious violations of international humanitarian law committed in the territory of Rwanda and Rwandan citizens responsible for such violations committed in the territory of neighboring States, between 1 January 1994 and 31 December 1994.

2. The Prosecutor shall act independently as a separate organ of the International Tribunal for Rwanda. He or she shall not seek or receive instructions from any Government or from any other source.

3. The Prosecutor of the International Tribunal for the Former Yugoslavia shall also serve as the Prosecutor of the International Tribunal for Rwanda. He or she shall have additional staff, including an additional Deputy Prosecutor, to assist with prosecutions before the International Tribunal for Rwanda. Such staff shall be appointed by the Secretary-General on the recommendation of the Prosecutor.

Article 16
The Registry

1. The Registry shall be responsible for the administration and servicing of the International Tribunal for Rwanda.

2. The Registry shall consist of a Registrar and such other staff as may be required.

3. The Registrar shall be appointed by the Secretary-General after consultation with the President of the International Tribunal for Rwanda. He or she shall serve for a four-year term and be eligible for reappointment. The terms and conditions of service of the Registrar shall be those of an Assistant Secretary-General of the United Nations.

4. The staff of the Registry shall be appointed by the Secretary-General on the recommendation of the Registrar.

Article 17
Investigation and preparation of the indictment

1. The Prosecutor shall initiate investigations ex-officio or on the basis of information obtained from any source, particularly from Governments, United Nations organs, intergovernmental and non-governmental organizations. The Prosecutor shall assess the information received or obtained and decide whether there is sufficient basis to proceed.

2. The Prosecutor shall have the power to question suspects, victims and witnesses, to collect evidence and to conduct on-site investigations. In carrying out these tasks, the Prosecutor may, as appropriate, seek the assistance of the State authorities concerned.

3. If questioned, the suspect shall be entitled to be assisted by counsel of his or her own choice, including the right to have legal assistance assigned to the suspect without payment by him or her in any such case if he or she does not have sufficient means to pay for it, as well as to necessary translation into and from a language he or she speaks and understands.

4. Upon a determination that a *prima facie* case exists, the Prosecutor shall prepare an indictment containing a concise statement of the facts and the crime or crimes with which the accused is charged under the Statute. The indictment shall be transmitted to a judge of the Trial Chamber.

Article 18
Review of the indictment

1. The judge of the Trial Chamber to whom the indictment has been transmitted shall review it. If satisfied that *prima facie* case has been established by the Prosecutor, he or she shall confirm the indictment. If not so satisfied, the indictment shall be dismissed.

2. Upon confirmation of an indictment, the judge may, at the request of the Prosecutor, issue such orders and warrants

for the arrest, detention, surrender or transfer of persons, and any others as may be required for the conduct of the trial.

Article 19
Commencement and conduct of trial proceedings

1. The Trial Chambers shall ensure that a trial is fair and expeditious and that proceedings are conducted in accordance with the rules of procedure and evidence, with full respect for the rights of the accused and due regard for protection of victims and witnesses.

2. A person against whom an indictment has been confirmed shall, pursuant to an order or and arrest warrant of the International Tribunal for Rwanda, be taken into custody, immediately informed of the charges against him or her and transferred to the International Tribunal for Rwanda.

3. The Trial Chamber shall read the indictment, satisfy itself that the rights of the accused are respected, confirm that the accused understands the indictment, and instruct the accused to enter a plea. The Trial Chamber shall then set the date for trial.

4. The hearings shall be public unless the Trial Chamber decides to close the proceedings in accordance with its rules of procedure and evidence.

Article 20
Rights of the accused

1. All persons shall be equal before the International Tribunal for Rwanda.

2. In the determination of charges against him or her, the accused shall be entitled to a fair and public hearing, subject to Article 21 of the Statute.

3. The accused shall be presumed innocent until proved guilty according to the provisions of the present Statute.

4. In the determination of any charge against the accused pursuant to the present Statute, the accused shall be entitled to the following minimum guarantees, in full equality:

   (a) To be informed promptly and in detail in a language which he or she understands of the nature and cause of the charge against him or her;

   (b) To have adequate time and facilities for the preparation of his or her defense and to communicate with counsel of his or her own choosing;

   (c) To be tried without undue delay;

   (d) To be tried in his or her presence, and to defend himself or herself in person or through legal assistance of his or her own choosing; to be informed, if he or she does not have legal assistance, of this right; and to have legal assistance assigned to him or her, in any case where the interests of justice so require, and without payment by him or her in any case if he or she does not have sufficient means to pay for it;

   (e) To examine, or have examined, the witnesses against him or her and to obtain the attendance and examination of witnesses on his or her behalf under the same conditions as witnesses against him or her;

   (f) To have the free assistance of an interpreter if he or she cannot understand or speak the language used in the International Tribunal for Rwanda;

   (g) Not to be compelled to testify against himself or herself or to confess guilt.

Article 21
Protection of victims and witnesses

The International Tribunal for Rwanda shall provide in its rules of procedure and evidence for the protection of victims and witnesses. Such protection measures shall include, but shall not be limited to, the conduct of in-camera proceedings and the protection of the victim's identity.

Article 22
Judgment

1. The Trial Chambers shall pronounce judgments and impose sentences and penalties on persons convicted of serious violations of international humanitarian law.

2. The judgment shall be rendered by a majority of the judges of the Trial Chamber, and shall be delivered by the Trial Chamber in public. It shall be accompanied by a reasoned opinion in writing, to which separate or dissenting opinions may be appended.

Article 23
Penalties

1. The penalty imposed by the Trial Chamber shall be limited to imprisonment. In determining the terms of imprisonment, the Trial Chambers shall have recourse to the general practice regarding prison sentence in the courts of Rwanda.

2. In imposing the sentences, the Trial Chambers should take into account such factors as the gravity of the offense and the individual circumstances of the convicted person.

3. In addition to imprisonment, the Trial Chambers may order the return of any property and proceeds acquired by criminal conduct, including by means of duress, to their rightful owners.

Article 24
Appellate proceedings

1. The Appellate Chamber shall hear appeals from persons convicted by the Trial Chambers or from the Prosecutor on the following grounds:

   (a) An error on a question of law invalidating the decision; or

(b) An error of fact which has occasioned a miscarriage of justice.

2. The Appeals Chamber may affirm, reverse or revise the decisions taken by the Trial Chambers.

Article 25
Review proceedings

Where a new fact has been discovered which was not known at the time of the proceedings before the Trial Chamber or the Appeals Chamber and which could have been a decisive factor in reaching the decision, the convicted person or the Prosecutor may submit to the International Tribunal for Rwanda an application for review of the judgment.

Article 26
Enforcement of sentences

Imprisonment shall be served in Rwanda or any of the States on a list of States which have indicated to the Security Council their willingness to accept convicted persons, as designated by the International Tribunal for Rwanda. Such imprisonment shall be in accordance with the applicable law of the State concerned, subject to the supervision of the International Tribunal for Rwanda.

Article 27
Pardon or commutation of sentences

If, pursuant to the applicable law of the State in which the convicted person is imprisoned, he or she is eligible for pardon or commutation of sentence, the State concerned shall notify the International Tribunal for Rwanda accordingly. There shall only be pardon or commutation of sentence if the President of the International Tribunal for Rwanda, in consultation with the judges, so decides on the basis of interests of justice and the general principles of law.

Article 28
Cooperation and judicial assistance

1. States shall cooperate with the International Tribunal for Rwanda in the investigation and prosecution of persons accused of committing serious violations of international humanitarian law.

2. States shall comply without undue delay with any request for assistance of an order issued by the Trial Chamber, including, but not limited to:

   (a) The identification and location of persons;

   (b) The taking of testimony and the production of evidence;

   (c) The service of documents;

   (d) The arrest and detention of persons;

   (e) The surrender or the transfer of the accused to the International Tribunal for Rwanda.

Article 29
The status, privileges and immunities of the International Tribunal for Rwanda

1. The Convention on the Privileges and Immunities of the United Nations of 13 February 1946 shall apply to the International Tribunal for Rwanda, the judges, the Prosecutor and his or her staff, and the Registrar and his or her staff.

2. The judges, the Prosecutor and the Registrar shall enjoy the privileges and immunities, exemptions and facilities accorded to diplomatic envoys, in accordance with international law.

3. The staff of the Prosecutor and of the Registrar shall enjoy the privileges and immunities accorded to officials of the United Nations under Articles V and VII of the Convention referred to in paragraph 1 of this article.

4. Other persons, including the accused, required at the seat or meeting place of the International Tribunal for Rwanda shall be accorded such treatment as is necessary for the proper functioning of the International Tribunal for Rwanda.

Article 30
Expenses of the
International Tribunal for Rwanda

The expenses of the International Tribunal for Rwanda shall be expenses of the Organization in accordance with Article 17 of the Charter of the United Nations.

Article 31
Working languages

The working languages of the International Tribunal shall be English and French.

Article 32
Annual report

The President of the International Tribunal for Rwanda shall submit an annual report of the International Tribunal for Rwanda to the Security Council and to the General Assembly.

Appendix II

October 1990	Attacks by Rwandan Patriotic Front (RPF) from bases in Uganda.
August 1993	President Juvenal Havyarimana and the RPF sign Arusha Peace Accords.
November 1993	United Nations (UN) forces arrive in Rwanda to monitor the progress of Arusha Peace Accords. The Accords fail to take effect.
6 April 1994	The plane carrying President Havyarimana of Rwanda and President Cyprien Ntanyamira of Burundi is shot down near Kigali Airport. This event triggers mass killings. Within hours, the Hutu army, in conjunction with Interahamwe, attack innocent ethnic Tutsi and moderate Hutu.
7 April 1994	Agathe Uwilingiyimana, the first woman Prime Minister, is tortured and shot to death. Her UN bodyguards face similar fates.
10 April 1994	Western embassies close their doors and evacuate their citizens.

21 April 1994	The UN Security Council cuts back its forces from 25 hundred to 270 troops.
29 April 1994	More than 500 thousand refugees flee to Tanzania within 24 hours.
23 June 1994	French military intervention.
4 July 1994	The RPF captures Kigali.
14 July 1994	One million refugees arrive in the Democratic Republic of the Congo (Zaire).
18 July 1994	The RPF declares a cease-fire. A new government is announced.
8 November 1994	The UN Security Council approves a resolution establishing an international court to try people accused of genocide in Rwanda.

Appendix III

1885-1886	Rwanda falls under the German sphere of influence at the Berlin Conference.
1908	Germany establishes military command in Rwanda.
1924	Rwanda becomes a mandate of Belgium after the First World War.
1931	The Belgian government deposes Mwami Musinga.
1959	Hutu revolution and Tutsi massacre.
1961	Abolition of Rwandan monarchy.
1962	Rwanda becomes an independent republic with Gregoire Kayibanda as its first Hutu president.
1963-1973	Unnoticed Tutsi pogroms.
1973	President Kayibanda is overthrown in a coup d'etat.

1988	The Rwandan Patriotic Front (RPF) is founded.
1990	The RPF attacks the government of Rwanda from Uganda.
1991	The government of Rwanda retaliates by massacring defenseless ethnic Tutsi within the country.
1993	The RPF offensive, French intervention, Arusha Peace Accords, and deployment of the United Nations Mission in Rwanda (UNAMIR).
1994	Airplane crash, death of President Juvenal Havyarimana, Tutsi genocide, evacuation of European and United States nationals, France's Operation Turquoise, the RPF offensive, Hutu exodus, unilateral cease-fire, withdrawal of French troops, deployment of United States' Operation Hope, and the fall of Kigali, Butare, Gitarama, and Gisenyi.

For UN related activities in Rwanda, consult Security Council Resolutions 719, 912, 918, 925, 929, and 935.

2

BURUNDI

President Melchior Ndadaye's[17] favorite slogan was "Burundi nouveau" (a new Burundi), reminiscent of Mwami Ntare V's slogan, "homme nouveau, ere nouvelle" (a new man, a new era). Both leaders met similar fates. They failed to understand an old Kirundi proverb, "Ntawuvuka rimwe ngo yuzure ingovyi" (It takes a while to grow up). Burundi was, Burundi is, and Burundi will always be. The past is not dead. It is not even past. The present links the past to a distant future. As the Old Testament reminds us, "There is nothing new under the sun."

In traditional Burundi culture, there is a tendency to ignore the past. The future is virtually nonexistent and the concept of time is silent or indifferent. The concept of time is patterned after the sun, moon, stars, harvesting seasons, climatic seasons, and animal and human activities.

The Kirundi word *ubu* (now) has a sense of immediacy, nearness, and oneness. It covers the immediate concern of the people. The word *kera* (past) overlaps with *ubu*. The word *ejo* may mean either yesterday or tomorrow depending on the context. Therefore, there is a general lack of contingency in planning and a tendency to react spontaneously on the actions of others.

TRADITIONAL BURUNDI

Nestled in the mountains of the moon, Burundi is characterized by an endless succession of hills and valleys. Its culture traces its history to the ancient Kemetic civilization. The legendary Nile has its source in Burundi. The Abarundi, like most Africans, are animists.[18] They believe in a supreme being—Imana.[19] Imana is the cause of all good things. Imana gives life and sustains life. Imana is often invoked in poems, tales, songs, proverbs, dialogues, and plays. Children are named after Imana (Nahimana, Niyukuri, Ngendakumana, Niyongere, Nsengayo, Habonimana, Bigirimana, and Bizimana).

Imana is believed to dwell in Isonga. From there he oversees the activities of the Abarundi. Imana is good and powerful. He gives joy, peace, and prosperity. Kiranga, an invisible spirit, carries Imana's commission and channels Imana's blessings. Kiranga plays a role comparable to that of Jesus Christ or Mohammed. He gives good things to those who obey and keeps evil spirits away from them. On a lower level, *abapfumu* play the role of Catholic priests, Protestant pastors, or Islamic imams.

Abapfumu are generally divided into three categories: *abavurati, abaterekezi,* and *abashitsi. Abavurati* are known as rainmakers. They are believed to be able to make or prevent rain and punish enemies by sending thunderbolts. *Abaterekezi* are the keepers of pythons. Believed to possess the magic of handling the most feared snakes, *abaterekezi* were the guardians of Abami burial sites. *Abashitsi*, the callers of the dead, are believed to have the power to connect the dead with the living in case of family difficulties.

Spirits of deceased *umwami* are believed to affect the entire nation. The Abarundi also believe in natural spirits, charms, totems, and taboos. Natural spirits are believed to dwell in rocks, valleys, streams, and forests. They occasionally appear in human form.

Imana's counterpart is Rwuba rwa Bigata. Rwuba rwa Bigata brings misfortune, sickness, crop failure, cattle epidemics, and fratricide. Rwuba rwa Bigata is believed to be a miscreator who spoils what Imana has made. He may be compared to the concept of Satan or the Devil.

According to legend, Imana created the first man on earth, Gihanga.[20] It is believed that Gihanga lived with Imana in the sky before falling to earth. Then Gihanga fathered three sons: Gatutsi, Gahutu, and Gatwa. (The legend fails to mention where he found his wife.) Gatutsi specialized in hunting; Gahutu specialized in soil science; and Gatwa specialized in pottery and entertainment.

After testing Gatutsi for bravery and courage, Gihanga gave him two royal drums: *karyenda* (male) and *mukakaryenda* (female). Gihanga instructed Gatutsi to rule over his brothers and their descendants.

Gihanga is also believed to have introduced cattle and sorghum, which are still the country's symbols of wealth and fertility.

The Abarundi are divided into three ethnic groups:[21] Abatutsi (descendants of Gatutsi), Abahutu (descendants of Gahutu), and Abatwa (descendents of Gatwa). The Abatutsi are believed to be descendants of Cush, the grandson of biblical Noah (Genesis 6:10).[22] They entered what is present day Burundi from Ethiopia and Somalia. Skillful in the art of warfare, they established the kingdoms of Ankole, Buha, Bunyamwezi, Burundi, and Rwanda. The Abatutsi also established a significant political hegemony in Lutshuru (a region now known as the Democratic Republic of the Congo). Their political and social organization was patterned after that of pharaonic Egypt.

Social anthropologists trace the origin of the Abatutsi to pre-mosaic Israelites who migrated to Egypt and then fled southward when the country was invaded by Libya in twelfth century B.C. Their descendants became the people we now know as Ethiopians, Gallas, Somalis, and Abahima. Those who fled westward became Peuls and Fulanis (Chad, Niger, Mali, Guinea, Senegal, and Gambia).

During 500 B.C., Greek historian Herodotus described the inhabitants of the Nile as "Les plus beaux et les plus grands hommes a la peau luisante et brillante" (the most beautiful, tallest, light-skinned people).

The Abatutsi are divided into clans. Some clans were considered better than others.[23] The family patriarch exercised prerogatives over any decision effecting the entire family. Of primary concern were land distribution, marriage arrangements, and other legal matters. His word is considered final.

Burundi was founded by Mwami Ntare Rushatsi Cambarantama in 1500 A.D.[24] He crossed the Muragarazi River with his army and defeated local chieftains. He gradually established himself as an uncontested Umwami w'Abarundi (King of Burundi). His descendents were the *abaganwa*, a group from which the *umwami* was chosen. Later, the traditional administrative system consisted of *abaganwa* assisted by *abatware*, *abarongozi*, and *abashingantahe*. The society was organized along a caste system consisting of a hierarchy of clans and ethnic groups:

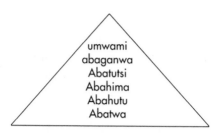

Social status was hereditary. Through marriage and individual merit, however, one could climb the social ladder.

The economic basis of the Abatutsi was essentially raising cattle. Cattle provided basic necessities such as milk, butter, meat, and hides. Hides were useful for clothing and mats. Cattle also provided dung for fertilizers. To the Umututsi, cattle were like money. They were considered a movable asset while the land was considered a fixed asset. Cattle were useful in acquiring clients who were obligated to assist their *shebuja* with manual work on the homestead, provide him with annual offerings in the form of sorghum or banana beers, and occasionally accompany him on distant journeys. In return, the *shebuja* was expected to protect his clients in legal and political matters. Such informal arrangements were not binding. Each contractor could arbitrarily end the relationship.

The Abahutu[25] were essentially engaged in food production, ironwork, weaving, woodcarving, basketry, and trading. Skillful in farming techniques and soil science, the Abahutu produced a variety of vegetable, fruit, grain, and root crops. They also raised goats, sheep, and chicken. Some Abahutu families were skillful craftsmen. They made clothes out of tree bark, designed and constructed traditional huts, and made household items. *Abapfumu, abavurati, abashitsi,* and *abaterekezi* practiced herbal medicine and became health care specialists.

The Abatwa are known as the original inhabitants of Burundi. As skillful manufacturers, the Abatwa made various household items and defense weapons. The Abatwa supplemented their income by hunting, gathering wild fruits, and entertaining at the royal court. Socially, however, they were discriminated against. Their physical appearances, mannerisms, and dialect were subject to ridicule.

Theoretically, *umwami* owned the land and cattle. *Abaganwa* considered *umwami* "first among equals." The Abatutsi gave tacit recognition and support to *umwami* but retained a great deal of independence. Justice was rendered in the name of *umwami*. *Karyenda*, a royal drum upon which hung the genitals of the vanquished, was a symbol of power. *Umwami* palaces were surrounded by a retinue of his followers, beautiful young women, and various visitors. Despite the absence of a standing army or police force, the *umwami* and his lieutenants were in a position to punish anyone who infringed on their prerogatives. Punishment could take the form of the disappropriation of one's cattle or land, or total banishment from the country. *Umwami* distributed social privileges according to individual merit, integrity, wisdom, and unblemished ethical standard. The dynastic abami names—Ntare (lion), Mwezi (moon), Mutaga (daylight), and Mwambutsa (crossing dangerous paths)—were recognized in sequences of unbroken line. Since Mwami Cambarantama founded Burundi five centuries ago (1500 A.D.), *umwami* were believed to be divine. *Abami* burial sites are believed to be sacred and guarded by pythons.

Before the advent of colonialism and a money economy, the concept of genocide in Burundian culture was alien. With outwardly friendly and gentle mannerisms, the Abarundi were the last people in the world to suspect of being capable of genocide. In cases of extreme family feuds, they resorted to psychological warfare against their opponents. Moreover, traditional weapons of defense, such as spears, bows, arrows, swords, and clubs, were not efficient for wholesale genocide. They were made for hunting or as a deterrent. Other household items, such as machetes and axes, were daily work tools.

GENOCIDE IN RWANDA AND BURUNDI IS AN OUTGROWTH OF COLONIALISM

Economic and political decisions affecting the country were made in Brussels with little regard to the needs and aspirations of the colonized or consultations with traditional hierarchy. Colonial objectives included the economic exploitation of the colonized, foreign-controlled education, and military intervention. These objectives were achieved through a triple alliance with the missionary, educator, and trader.

The Role of the Missionary

In the name of Christianity, missionaries accompanied military expeditions with a gun in one hand and the Bible in the other. As President of Kenya Jomo Kenyatta once remarked, "They gave us the Bible and they took the land." The so-called African elite has been trained in Catholic and Protestant missionaries ever since their establishment.

The role of the missionary was to attack and destroy traditional beliefs—the African soul—and to create in the African mind a state of self-doubt and low self-esteem. Catholic and Protestant missionaries competed for converts. The ruling class was converted first and the flock followed.[26]

Catholic teachings in Africa were executed to the letter. Sunday was declared *venerabilis di solis* (Council of Laodecia, 364 A.D.). Converts were forced to worship images of Jesus Christ, the Virgin Mary, and patron Saints (Second Council of Nicea, 787 A.D.). Catholic totems and rituals such as medals, rosaries, holy water, incense, novinas, candle burning, and confessional boxes replaced traditional African religious objects. Resistance to Catholic teachings was considered heresy and severely punished (Pope Innocent Edict of 1487; Council of Trent of 1545). Burundi's *abapfumu* were hunted and imprisoned; their religious objects confiscated and publicly burned. Reading or possession of the Bible was strictly forbidden (Council Tolosanum; Council of Toulouse, 1229). Mass was said in Latin. Promising young men and women were lured into convents and monasteries. Inter-marriage between Catholics and non-Catholics was forbidden.

The Christian myth of Original Sin tormented the illiterate population. The prospect of being sentenced to hell was unbearable. The promise of eternal life was enticing. The occasional sinner was promised a suspended sentence in purgatory. The White priest was mistakenly identified with Jesus Christ and became the key to salvation. Only through him may a sinner hope to reach the Kingdom of Heaven. Many cases of homosexuality and sexual assault were recorded.

The Role of the Educator

The role of the educator was to separate the student from his past—to destroy and deny him his history, culture, myth, legends, and traditions. In the cases of Rwanda and Burundi, the missionary played the dual role of evangelist and educator. The missionary was also expected to promote capitalist values such as acquisitiveness, cut-throat competition, and individualism.

The Role of the Trader

The role of the trader was to market European goods and create new tastes. Money, the new means of exchange, was obtainable by providing cheap labor or cheaply producing cash crops. In Burundi the people were forced to produce coffee while neglecting the production of basic food necessities. Those who resisted were punished with eight slashes.

Markets with Greek and Arab shops sprang up around colonial centers. Africans sold agricultural products and artifacts. African products were sold cheaply and imported goods were bought at high prices. As a result, expatriates became richer while the indigenous population became further entrenched in poverty. Traditional industries gradually lost their markets and slowly disappeared. As colonialism progressed, the new money economy began to transform basic social relationships. Once a self-sufficient community, the country was transformed into a dependent society.

The Belgian government instituted a head tax, cattle tax, and extra-wife tax. Colonial agents moved from village to village menacing citizens for taxes in a society with no money economy. Some young women who were on the verge of losing their lovers and husbands because of the new capitalistic demands devised the following lyric song:

Ntukaje i Kongo, Kongo ni mbare
Haja uwagowe, Yabuze ikori
Rya Sirikare, Hariri Nawe
Hariri We (bis)

Translation:

> *Do not go to the Congo*
> *Only a miserable person*
> *Who does not have money to pay government tax*
> *Goes to the Congo*

Young men left their villages in search of employment. They traveled to the nearby British colonies of Uganda and Tanganyika, where the shilling was much stronger than the Belgian franc. Seasonal workers returned to their villages with some savings but a substantial portion settled in their respective host countries.

Mwami Mwambutsa's Regime

Disappointed Hutu leaders attempted a coup on 19 October 1965. Prime Minister Leopold Bihumugani and Mwami Mwambutsa IV Bangiricenge escaped to Uvira unharmed. Twelve Tutsi officers at Camp Athenee were mercilessly murdered. By early morning the coup had failed and Michele Micombero, then Chief of Staff, emerged as a national hero. Mwami Mwambutsa IV issued a royal decree authorizing the execution of Hutu leaders by firing squad.[27] Soon thereafter he left for Switzerland with no intention of returning.

Execution of the Hutu leaders provoked a Hutu rebellion in Muramvya Province, a traditional fief of Mwami Mwambutsa IV. Armed with spears, bows, and arrows, Hutu hoodlums massacred Tutsi men, women, and children.[28] Government reprisals were equally severe. Ntavyibuha, the governor of Muramvya, is reported to have threatened a Hutu, "Uriruka ndakurase, uhagarare ndakurase" (You run, I shoot you, you stop, I shoot you). The 1965 coup became a prelude to endless inter-ethnic conflict. The social fabric had been ruptured.

Mwami Ntare V's Regime (July 1966-November 1996)

Little can be said of the last *mwami* of Burundi. Perhaps his fate had been sealed from the heavens. Against his father's wishes, the young and naïve Charles Ndizeye[29] declared himself Mwami Ntare V. He had allowed himself to be used as a pawn in a dangerous chess game.

Unlike his half-brother, Prince Louis Rwagasore,[30] Mwami Ntare V's only asset was his birthright.

His catch phrase "hommes nouveaux, ere nouvelle" was not convincing enough. "Ere nouvelle" ended within three months.

He returned from Europe and landed in Uganda in 1972. The presence of Mwami Ntare V in Uganda triggered President Micombero to request his extradition. In a letter to President Amin, President Micombero wrote:

> Just like you, I deeply believe in God. Your Excellency can be assured that as soon as Mr. Charles Ndizeye [Mwami Ntare V] returns back to my country, he will be considered as an ordinary citizen and as such, his life and security will be assured.[31]

The letter was hand-delivered by Foreign Minister Arthemon Simbananiye. Mwami Ntare V, now rendered powerless, was flown to Bujumbura, arrested, and imprisoned in Kitega. He was executed during the night uprisings in 1972 and buried with common criminals in a mass grave in Inyambeho, near the Catholic Mission of Giheta.

PRESIDENT MICHEL MICOMBERO'S REGIME (1966-1976)

Michel Micombero's[32] regime was characterized by extreme political instability and inter-ethnic tensions. A series of coups and counter-coups occurred. An alleged Hutu plot was discovered in 1969. As a result, Hutu civilian and military leaders were executed.[33] In 1972 an alleged Tutsi-led coup (Jenda-Muramvya axis) was discovered. A score of Tutsi leaders were arrested and imprisoned. Some were sentenced to death, though the death sentences were later commuted.[34]

On 29 April 1972, between 9 and 10 P.M., a band of ten thousand Hutu hoodlums attacked Bujumbura, Rumonge, Nyanza-Lac, and Bururi, hacking to death every Tutsi in sight.[35] They were heavily drugged and armed with machetes, spears, bows, arrows, and small fire arms. Like the Simbas during the 1964 Congo rebellion, the rebels believed themselves to be bulletproof. Similar attacks were repeated throughout the country. Government reprisals were equally severe.

Hutu civilian and military leaders were executed, including Martin Ndayahoze, Pascal Bubiriza, and Marc Ndayiziga.[36] Thousands more Hutu fled to Rwanda, Tanzania, and the Democratic Republic of the Congo (Zaire).[37] Though victorious, Micombero's regime was left crippled. He was overthrown while in a state of drunkenness in 1976.[38]

PRESIDENT JEAN-BAPTISTE BAGAZA'S REGIME (1976-1987)

During President Bagaza's[39] regime there were few disturbances. Perceived and misperceived threats were swiftly crushed. His government concentrated on development projects such as drinking water, electrification, housing, and road construction.

Improving on Micombero's political ingenuity, Bagaza ordered legislative elections in which he handpicked seventy-five percent of the candidates and appointed twenty-five percent more. His rubber-stamp lawmaking body never made any laws. Meanwhile, the autocratic President Bagaza consolidated himacracy. President Bagaza was finally overthrown while attending the Francophone Conference in Montreal, Canada. His right-hand man, Isidore Nyaboya,[40] was thrown in jail.

PRESIDENT PIERRE BUYOYA'S REGIME

President Buyoya's[41] regime was characterized by a series of spontaneous Hutu outbursts which led to the 1988 Ntega-Marangara massacres. The Ntega-Marangara incident was triggered by a minor coffee trade dispute between a Tutsi merchant and a Hutu trader. The underlying cause was the sad memory of 1972 and general political malaise. Tutsi phobia had become a serious psychological problem. The very sight of a Tutsi in military uniform caused fear and flight.

As before, Hutu hoodlums attacked every Tutsi in sight. Nearby Catholic churches were transformed into death camps. Government reprisals were equally severe.[42] Thousands perished and thousands more fled to Rwanda.

Under domestic and international pressure, President Buyoya appointed ethnic Hutu to important ministerial positions and undertook reforms. He initiated a democratization process in an undemocratic environment. A liberal constitution was written and overwhelmingly approved in a national referendum. Election laws were enacted and a multi-party system was legalized. International king-makers hailed the Buyoya regime as a model of democracy. As in "Le Corbeau et le Renard," President Buyoya himself began to believe that he had succeeded:

> *Que vous êtes joli, que vous me semble beau,*
> *Sans mentir si votre ramage se resemble a votre plumage;*
> *Vous êtes le phoenix des hotes de ces bois.*
> *A ces mots, le corbeau ne se sent pas de joie,*
> *Mais pour montrer sa belle voix,*
> *Il ouvre un large bec et laisse tomber son fromage.*
> *Le renard s'en saisit et dit:*
> *Mon bon monsieur, apprenez que tout flatteur*
> *Vit au depens de celui qui l'écoute.*

Translation:

> *The Crow and the Fox*
> *Master Crow, perched in a tree,*
> *Held in his beak a piece of cheese*
> *Master Fox, attracted by the smell, said:*
> *"Aha! Good morning, Mr. Crow*
> *How handsome you look*
> *How gorgeous your feathers are*
> *Honestly, you are the phoenix of this woodland!"*
> *At these words, the crow tried to run a few scales*
> *Opened his huge beak and dropped his cheese*
> *The Fox pounced on it and made a remark*
> *"My dear sir, learn that every flatterer*
> *Lives at the expense of his listener."*[43]

President Melchior Ndadaye's Regime (July 1993-October 1993)

Motivated by a deep hatred for the Tutsi-dominated army and the 1972 massacre, the Hutu overwhelmingly voted for *Front pour la democracy au Burundi* (FRODEBU). The 1993 elections were unique in that they aimed directly at the executive branch of government. Previously, *abami* claimed divine right. Their military successors gained power through the barrel of the gun. In each case, the population stoically accepted the outcome.

During his short rule, President Ndadaye made four important decisions which are believed to have ultimately led to his final demise:

1. In what appeared to be a populist move, but essentially calculated to divide the army, he granted a blanket amnesty. More than five hundred political prisoners were freed. Thousands of refugees, some of them trained in guerrilla warfare, returned home and menaced peaceful citizens. Former President Bagaza returned from Libya.

2. He dismissed senior government officials.

3. He announced his intention to create a separate police force and to retire senior military officers.

4. He announced his intention to amend the Constitution and abolish the traditional institution of *ubushingantahe* (wise men and judges).

Like Buyoya, President Ndadaye also naïvely believed in democracy. His ascendancy to power had no military backing. During a meeting with *la Communaute Burundaise* at the New York Plaza Hotel in the United States,[44] he spoke about democracy. His catch phrase was "homme nouveau." He was probably aware that his days were numbered.

Democracy is not just calling for elections. Democracy cannot be decreed or imported. It is a state of mind. It requires psychological transformation. In developing countries, democracy is a volatile concept. As one Algerian politician correctly observed, "One man, one vote, one time." When Algerian fundamentalist Muslims won a legislative election, the military government voided the election. The Nigerian military government voided presidential elections. In Burundi the military assassinated the first elected Hutu president. In Angola elections triggered a renewal of civil war. In Haiti elections brought power to an unstable priest.

President Ndadaye's policies of proportional representation in schools, army, and employment in the public sector irritated ethnic Tutsi. They regrouped against what they perceived to be arrogant and threatening Hutu behavior. Moreover, rumors of the Hutu Minister of Interior purchasing machetes was interpreted as a preparation for Tutsi massacre.

On 21 October 1993 at 2 A.M., a para-commando tank unit attacked the presidential palace and the radio-television station. President

Ndadaye and his family were taken to Camp Muha. He was separated from his family and transferred to a para-commando camp where he was beaten, stabbed, and had his head crushed. Several of President Ndadaye's political associates also lost their lives. Euzebia Nshimirimana, the spouse of Sylvestre Ntibantunganya, then the Minister of Foreign Affairs (now a former president), was bayoneted to death. The rest of President Ndadaye's government sought refuge in Belgian, French, and Rwandan embassies. The French Embassy staff complained about the smell of their Hutu guests and transferred them to the fish-smelling guest house near Lake Tanganyika under French guard.

President Ndadaye's death triggered the Tutsi genocide. Hutu leaders called on Hutu masses to exterminate ethnic Tutsi:

- Minister of Health Dr. Jean Minani (Dr. Mengele of Burundi) called on the Hutu to stand firm.

- Minister of Labor Leonard Nyangoma called for the dismantling of Burundi's army.

- Minister of Transportation Schadrack Niyonkuru called for the burning of every moving vehicle.

- Minister of Foreign Affairs Paul Munyembari called for "an eye for an eye, a tooth for a tooth," meaning a dead Tutsi for a dead Hutu.

- Governor of Gitega Johachin Nabwera called on the Hutu to be alert and not allow the enemy to escape.

- Governor of Muramvya Leonce Ndarubangiye called on the Hutu to block the roads, be vigilantes, refuse new leaders, and spread the news everywhere.

- Governor of Muyinga Barthazar Ndimurwanko called on masses of Hutu to destroy bridges, block roads, and not allow a Tutsi, a Hutu of *Union et progres nationale* (UPRONA), or a soldier to pass.

- The Governor of Bubanza divided the population into "group Hutu" and "group Tutsi" and ordered "group Hutu" to massacre "group Tutsi."

- Administrator of Muryansoro Andre Baryimare personally supervised the Tutsi massacre and strangled an elderly Tutsi woman.

- Administrator of Bubanza Roger Mayoya hacked a Tutsi judge and officially declared that he was beginning a campaign to exterminate the Tutsi.

The Hutu responded accordingly. Hutu hoodlums took revenge on innocent Tutsi throughout the countryside. Armed with machetes, spears, knives, and clubs, they roamed from village to village and house to house, hacking every Tutsi in sight. Churches and schools were transformed into killing fields:

- At Lycée de Kibimba, Director Firmat Niyonkenguruka, told his Tutsi students to go and be burned as they were not his. Tutsi teachers were captured, tied up, locked in nearby buildings, and set on fire. Sixty Tutsi perished. Kibimba has since been baptized the "Auschwitz of Burundi."

- At Lycée de Buhiga, Fidele Ndikumwami told Hutu students to leave and join their brothers. Then he ordered the slaughter of the Tutsi students.

- At Lycée de Ruyigi, Gaudence Munero (a Hutukazi) is reported to have shouted that she was going to take care of Tutsi women.

- In Mubimbi Hutu squads blocked the roads, grouped ethnic Tutsi together, and slaughtered them. Later, in a letter demanding payment, acting President Ntaryamira was implicated.

- In Bukeye, Kiganda, Rutegama, and Inyabihanga,[45] the Tutsi had their hands tied behind their backs and hacked to death. Corpses were left rotting along the streets.

- In Kayanza, Ngozi, and Kirundo Provinces, ethnic Tutsi were decapitated and burned alive. In one dramatic incident, a Tutsi judge was sliced to death and his heart was barbecued for an evening meal. The rest were thrown into the Akanyaru River.

- In Bugendana, Mutaho, Giheta, Makebuko, Mwanzari, Bukirasazi, and Gishubi,[46] ethnic Tutsi were tortured, mutilated, decapitated, and crucified. Some of the victims were thrown into the Ruvubu and Ruvyironza Rivers.

- In Butezi, Butaganzwa, Rusengo, and Muriza, ethnic Tutsi were wiped out. The family of Clavera, the spouse of an Anglican Bishop, Pie Ntukamazina, was decimated. Cajetan Rugambarara, an elderly former Supreme Court Justice, was hacked and left for dead. He survived to tell the tales.

- In Rutana Province,[47] ethnic Tutsi had their hands tied behind their back and were hacked to death.

Similar calls were repeated throughout the country. Tutsi men had their hands bound and were thrown into the Ruvubu, Ruvyironza, and Akanyaru Rivers. Women were raped and slaughtered. Students were locked in buildings and then set afire. Churches became the killing fields. Some were even murdered by hand-to-hand strangulation. Tutsi houses were burned. Cattle were cut into pieces. Bodies were left rotting along the streets. To prevent military intervention, roads were blocked with trees, bridges were destroyed, and telephones lines were cut.

This type of guerrilla warfare cannot be interpreted as a spontaneous response of illiterate Hutu peasants or functionally illiterate FRODEBU leaders alone. The Tutsi genocide was planned and financed well in advance by neo-colonial interests. In the September 1993 *Africa Report* interview with President Ndadaye, the article insinuated that if he were assassinated, every Tutsi family will lose at least one of its members. It happened. FRODEBU leaders applied Rwanda's plan in Burundi. Six months later, similar methods, tactics, and strategies were repeated in Rwanda. The objective was extermination of ethnic Abatutsi.

In a letter written by genocidal squads demanding payment and published in *le Carefour des idees* (1994), President Cyprien Ntaryamira[48] was implicated, "Mwahevye bamwe, natwe ntiduhumga mutaduhaye. Zana ayo mahera, muduhe ibihumbi cumi umwe umwe" (You paid some, we are not going to flee without being paid. Give us money, each ten thousands).

President Sylvestre Ntibantunganya's Regime (1994-1996)

If Buyoya's regime is characterized by naïveté, Ntibantunganya's[49] regime is characterized by an uneasy ethnic coalition and extreme incompetence. According to the Kigobe Agreements, a Hutu-dominated FRODEBU retained the presidency, and a Tutsi-dominated UPRONA retained executive power. Ministerial and ambassadorial positions were apportioned among various political parties but executive powers otherwise reserved for the president gravitated toward Chief of Staff Jean Bikomagu. FRODEBU leaders were either forced to resign or were placated. The rest went into exile.

Hutu death squads under the aegis of the National Council for the Defense of Democracy (CNDD) led by Leonard Nyangoma[50] and financed by neo-colonial interests, stepped up an anti-Tutsi campaign of terrorism and murder. Kamenge, now known as "Little Beirut," and other suspected Hutu hideouts were cleansed. The cataclysm occurred on 20 July 1996. Hutu hoodlums armed with guns, machetes, spears, and clubs massacred 340 internally displaced Tutsi in Bugendana and burned the refugee camp. At the funeral of the victims an angry crowd threw rocks and cow dung at the president and spit on him, a cultural sign of extreme anger. Frightened, President Ntibantunganya sought refuge in the United States Embassy. Other Hutu ministers sought refuge in the German Embassy. It was President Ntibantunganya's second time seeking protection in a foreign embassy. During the abortive coup of 1993, he sought refuge in the French Embassy.

On 25 July 1996 the army officially announced the coup. Soldiers in combat camouflage, paratroopers in maroon berets, and commandos in green berets manned Bujumbura. Road blocks were set up. Borders and the airport were sealed off. A 7:00 P.M. curfew was declared. Political parties were banned and military leaders nominated Buyoya to assume the presidency again.

President Buyoya reiterated the old story that there is "no Hutu no Tutsi, but one people." It sounded like the American motto "E pluribus unum." He rationalized the military coup to be an act to save a people in distress and to stop repeated massacres. Then he appealed to the international community, "We demand that international community understands the purpose of our efforts. What happened today is an act of salvation . . . ." He praised President Mwalima Julius Kamparage Nyerere of Tanzania for his efforts to broker an internal peace. A military spokesman's statement was more revealing, "We don't care if the Hutu see this as green light or war. We are going to fight them properly."[51]

The country's political landscape seemed to be disintegrating into two nations—one Hutu and another Tutsi—as if they were living on separate planets.

INTERNATIONAL REACTION TO BURUNDI COUPS OF 1993 AND 1996

Ever since the 1959 Belgian-assisted Tutsi genocide in Rwanda, Euro-United States policies have been consistently and conveniently sympathetic with Hutu racist genocidal politics in Burundi. The underlying reasons are still not clear.

The 1993 elections were planned, financed, coordinated, and supervised by neo-colonial interests in the name of New World Order (Disorder). As their brainchild succeeded, Burundi became an overnight international role model of a successful democracy. To a capitalist, democracy means a market economy. The World Bank promised to increase loans. Western powers promised to increase economic assistance. Meanwhile, the French government sought military bases in Burundi.

Within twenty-four hours of the attempted coup, a diplomatic chain-reaction took place in Western capitals. Western countries immediately announced the suspension of economic aid. The UN Security Council condemned the coup. Western press corps reported the coup as a failed democracy—an imaginary democracy which does not exist, never existed, and will never exist as long as human nature remains the same.

As Hutu carnage continued on the beautiful hills of Burundi, the UN Security Council remained silent instead of condemning the Tutsi genocide under Articles II and III (b), (c), (d), and (e) of the UN Convention on the Prevention and Punishment of the Crime of Genocide.

United Nations

UN Secretary-General Boutros Boutros-Ghali reacted to the July 1996 coup[52] by condemning it. The UN Security Council threatened to send a multinational contingency force. UN Secretary-General Boutros-Ghali had recommended in his letter to the UN Security Council a preventive diplomacy in which a rapid reaction force could be stationed in the Democratic Republic of the Congo (Zaire). He stressed that a real danger of the situation in Burundi was degenerating to the point where it might explode into ethnic violence on massive scale.

The preventive diplomacy did not materialize. Familiar questions were asked again: Who is contributing peacekeeping forces? For what purpose? How long? Who will pay? The UN Security Council threatened to send a multinational contingency force in accordance with Chapters VI and VII of the UN Charter, but the concept of national sovereignty was also a problem.

United States Ambassador to the UN Madeleine Albright (currently serving as United States Secretary of State in the Clinton Administration), was categorical:

> Under no circumstances would we tolerate a government installed by force or intimidation. The cycle of violence must cease. Extremists cannot be allowed to set up an agenda.[53]

But the Belgian Foreign Minister's statement was cautious, "Given the situation now, it is possible that Buyoya is the least of evils."[54] The presence of President Buyoya at the political scene quieted Western capitals.

Organization of African Unity (OAU)

While Western capitals toned down their criticisms of the coup in Burundi, Africans "cried wolf." The ambassador of Botswana, a country whose police force is equipped with nightsticks, called for the removal of President Buyoya. The OAU committee meeting in Arusha,[55] chaired by President Nyerere,[56] condemned the coup. They called for reinstating parliament and lifting the ban on political parties. They also discussed the possibility of a multinational military intervention.[57] Soon thereafter, Tanzania and Kenya declared an economic embargo.[58]

CONCLUSION

Burundi's cycle of violence during the past three decades has become endemic. Since ascending to independence, Burundi has experienced six *coups d'états*. Out of nine leaders, three have been assassinated.[59] Unending inter-ethnic civil strife has left thousands dead.

Thousands of articles and a few books have been written about Burundi's problems, and statements have been made in both national and international forums—but it seems that there are no solutions in sight. The following proposals have already been mentioned:

1. Delineation of ethnic districts within the country.

2. Separate ethnic states (Rwanda for the Hutu and Burundi for the Tutsi, or vice versa).

3. UN military intervention (to keep apart inter-ethnic interaction).

4. Economic sanctions (to force ethnic Tutsis to give up power).

5. Total demilitarization of Burundi (like Switzerland, Costa Rica, Botswana, and Haiti, in order to emasculate the Tutsi).

The above proposals are as close to utopian as possible. Any attempt to displace a population from its natural environment is likely to fail. UN peacekeeping operations have never been effective anywhere, with the exception of Cyprus. The solution lies in the heads of both ethnic Hutus and Tutsis. If we lived side by side peacefully for more than five centuries, we can live together now and forever. There is no mono-ethnic nation anywhere in the world.

MODERN BURUNDI DIPLOMATIC HISTORY

Diplomacy is the art of conducting relations among sovereign nations. The objectives of diplomacy are to promote cooperation among economic and cultural interests. Treaties on trade, defense, and cultural exchanges are made by interested parties. Nations are expected to observe the instruments of international law in times of peace as well as in time of war. Often, however, treaties are either suspended, broken, or overlooked. Then the principle of "might makes right" prevails.

During the pre-colonial era Burundi conducted its foreign relations with Rwanda, Buha, and Karagwe through a network of cunning spies. These spies collected information on the military and political situations of perceived enemies. Since there were no formal embassies, consulates, or legations, the word of the king was final. Military alliances were concluded spontaneously.

At the Berlin Conference of 1884-85, Burundi fell under the German sphere of influence. In 1890 the country officially became part of the German-East African Empire, encompassing Tanganyika (Tanzania), Rwanda, and Burundi.[60] German Junkers were fiercely resisted by Burundi's traditional army, Intwaramiheto, until 1903. Mwami Mwezi Gisabo[61] hoped to decisively defeat the German army as he had previously done against the Arab slave trader, Rumaliza (Muhammed). But the traditional weapons consisting of spears and bows and arrows proved inefficient against German rifles.

Defeated, Mwami Gisabo reluctantly agreed to sign the Treaty of Kiganda on 6 August 1903. In return, Germany agreed to recognize him as Mwami of Burundi and helped him defeat his rivals.[62] Shortly after his return from a reception at the German military headquarters in Usumbura, Mwami Gisabo mysteriously died. His young son, Mutaga Mbikije, succeeded him to the throne. A few years later, he too mysteriously died. He was succeeded by his younger son Mwami Mwambutsa IV Bangiricenge. Political power had reverted to his uncles and grandmother, Ririkumutima. The German Reich ruled Burundi until the end of the First World War. Burundi was handed over to Belgium as a mandate and later converted into a United Nations (UN) trusteeship.

After independence, Mwami Mwambutsa IV assumed the country's diplomatic relations. Previously, Louis Rwagasore's UPRONA had closely collaborated with Patrice Lumumba's *Mouvement nationale Congolais* (MNC), Nyerere's Tanganyika National Union (TANU), and Rwanda's *Union nationale Rwandaise* (UNAR). It was logical for these organizations to coordinate their foreign relations after independence. Unforeseeable events, however, changed the course of regional politics.

Lumumba and Rwagasore were prematurely assassinated. UNAR was defeated and Tutsi genocide in Rwanda took its toll.

The illiterate Mwami Mwambutsa IV was not in any position to grasp the complexities and intricacies of modern diplomacy. Neither were his close advisors.[63] Instead, his foreign policy followed the old adage "the enemy of my enemy is my friend, and the friend of my enemy is my enemy." He failed to understand that in "real politik" there are neither permanent friends nor permanent enemies, but permanent interests. Young Western-educated Tutsi Turks flirted with Marxism while young Hutus drifted toward Kayibandism.

REGIONAL DIPLOMACY

Rwanda

Rwanda and Burundi are like identical twins. They share identical ethnic composition, history, culture, and language. Like identical twins, if one is sick the other becomes sick, too. Ideally, both countries should have become one country at best, federated at worst. But events leading to independence caused them to drift apart. In 1991 when the Rwandan Patriotic Front (RPF) crossed the border from Uganda and threatened Kigali, President Juvenal Havyarimana accused President Yoweri Museveni of having an agenda to create an empire in the region and embarked on a policy of regional "Hutization." He encouraged a Hutu invasion of Burundi. Hutu attacks in 1990, 1991, and 1992 provoked undue rupture of diplomatic relations. The mysterious plane crash on 6 April 1994 in which both presidents of Burundi and Rwanda lost their lives led to the "final solution."

Tanzania

Burundi shares with Tanzania traditional cultural affinity, geographical contiguity, and past Swahili and German colonial legacy. During the British colonial era, Burundians trekked to Tanganyika (Tanzania) in search of employment and remained there. The influx of refugees in the early 1970s often created diplomatic nuisances between the two countries. In 1973, the Burundian army mistakenly killed Tanzanian citizens, an incident that caused a temporarily blockade.[64]

The Democratic Republic of the Congo (Zaire)

Burundi and the Democratic Republic of the Congo (Zaire) share geographic contiguity and a legacy of Belgian colonialism. During the early years of independence, Prime Minister Lumumba flirted with the idea of annexing both Rwanda and Burundi. After Prime Minister Lumumba's assassination the Burundian government sided with Lumumbist factions and flirted with the Communist bloc. Prime Minister Tshombe retaliated by sacking the Burundi Embassy in Leopoldville and cutting off the electricity in Bujumbura. Diplomatic relations were temporarily suspended. In 1966 Mwami Ntare V was overthrown while attending the first anniversary of Joseph Desiré Mobutu Sese Seko's coup. Mobutu intervened in Burundi's ethnic wars in 1972.

Uganda

Burundi maintains special diplomatic relations with Uganda. Both countries share a similar traditional culture. The former kingdoms of Ankole, Buganda, and Toro were organized along feudal systems similar to that of both Rwanda and Burundi. During British colonial rule many Burundian citizens migrated to Uganda in search of employment. Almost a half-million Burundians live and work in Uganda. Some of Burundi's imports pass through Uganda to and from Mombasa, a Kenyan port. King Mutesa II of Buganda sought asylum in Bujumbura while in transit to exile in London in 1965. President Idi Amin, in collusion with President Micombero, kidnapped and extradited Mwami Ntare V to Burundi. He was subsequently murdered on 30 October 1972. Upon his downfall, President Bagaza sought asylum in Uganda before embarking to his final exile in Libya in 1987. Afterwards, President Buyoya's regime sought friendly relations with President Museveni. The Permanent Mission of Burundi to the UN began to function as if it was a Ugandan interest section. Burundi also maintains diplomatic relations with Algeria, Egypt, Kenya, and Ethiopia.

DIPLOMATIC RELATIONS WITH INDUSTRIALIZED COUNTRIES

Diplomatic relations between developed and underdeveloped countries take the form of a donor-recipient relationship. Paradoxically, both the donor and recipient accept the development theory that foreign aid will stimulate economy in a linear fashion through capital accumulation.

Foreign aid may be in the form of long-term loans, soft loans, grants, sale of surplus, or subsidized products. Throughout the 1970s and 1980s, the advocates of the development theory were disappointed. The gap between the donors and recipients widened. The rich became richer and the poor became poorer. The recipient countries realized that foreign aid was not designed for economic development, but as a tool to promote the donor's foreign policies and to have leverage in the domestic policies of the recipient. The loans were often made with the provision that the recipient use the funds to purchase equipment and goods from the donor, and to be used as an outlet for employment for the donor's nationals. In other words, the money never left the donor's pocket. The development theory led to underdevelopment.

Europe

In the case of Burundi, Belgium has played a paternalistic role in providing economic and military assistance. Belgium trains most of Burundi's nationals in almost every field. Twenty-five percent of Burundi's budget is provided by Belgium. The Burundian government agrees to purchase goods and services from Belgium in return. Belgian trade, investments, and its co-operants receive preferential treatment. Thus, Belgian economic and military assistance proves to be another way to subsidize its own industries at home and create employment overseas for its otherwise unemployable nationals.

The Belgium ambassador to Burundi often acted as if he was a colonial governor by interfering in the choice of the country's leadership. In 1965 Ambassador Henniquiaux was implicated in the abortive coup against Mwami Mwambutsa IV. The Belgium Embassy was instrumental in the 1972 attempted genocide, and again in 1993. Both coups failed and Belgium reacted by cutting economic and military assistance. Burundi also maintains diplomatic relations with France, Germany, Italy, Switzerland, Russia, England, Sweden, and Romania. The Vatican maintains and finances a network of Roman Catholic churches and hospitals. Through Papal Nuncio, the Catholic Church exerts undue influence on government officials.

As Belgian fortunes declined, France began to act as a substitute in the former Belgian colonies. France provides economic and military assistance to the Democratic Republic of the Congo (Zaire), Rwanda, and Burundi. The French Embassy played an important role in the planning and financing of the 1993 Burundi elections. President Ndadaye's wife and children found refuge in the French Embassy after his assassination. The rest of President Ndadaye's cabinet was protected by French military personnel.

The United States

With the exception of Liberia, the United States was the least known of the developed countries in Africa. Information about the United States was brought to Africa through a network of Protestant missions.[65] When Burundi became independent in 1962, United States President John F. Kennedy sent a gift to Mwami Mwambutsa IV. It was a record player and some records. President Kennedy had heard of the king's midnight twisting expertise. Soon after, the American Embassy became an imposing structure in the center of Bujumbura. A few students were awarded scholarships to study in American colleges and universities (including this writer). Mwami Mwambutsa IV was invited to attend the 1964 New York World Fair with his famous dancers. Burundian deputies were invited to visit the United States. Step by step, Burundi was discovering the United States. Trade relations between the two countries are essentially limited to Arabica Coffee which is imported by the Folgers Company of Kansas, United States. Coffee represents approximately sixty percent of the country's foreign exchange.

During the Congo crisis, however, the Burundian government annoyed the United States by siding with the Sino-Soviet bloc. The American Embassy kidnapped Chinese Cultural Attaché Tung Chi-Ping (nicknamed Charlie). In August Tung Chi-Ping appeared before the United States Senate Foreign Relations Committee to testify on Chinese Communist subversion. In 1965 Ambassador Donald Dumont was implicated in the attempted coup and declared *persona non-grata.* Diplomatic relations were temporarily suspended. In 1972 Ambassador Patrick Melady was implicated in the attempted coup and quietly transferred to Uganda. In 1993 Ambassador Krugger was implicated in the planning and financing of elections. He was quietly transferred to Botswana. Burundi maintains friendly relations with Canada.

Asia

Diplomatic relations with Asia were immediately established after gaining independence. The Chinese government invited Burundian deputies to visit China and learn about the achievements of Mao's revolution. Mwami Mwambutsa IV was suspicious of Chinese intentions. He knew that Marxism was incompatible with a monarchy. Rumors persisted that the Chinese Embassy was involved in the 1965 assassination of Prime Minister Ngendandumwe. Mwami Mwambutsa IV reacted by expelling Chinese Ambassador Liu Yu Feng. Diplomatic relations were suspended until 1971. Burundi maintains diplomatic relations with North Korea, Japan, and Saudi Arabia.

Multilateral Diplomacy

Since the Berlin Conference, Burundi has been involved in international diplomatic relations. Through the Orts-Milner Agreement and the Treaty of Versailles, Burundi became a League of Nations mandate. After the Second World War the mandate was converted into a UN trusteeship. Since its independence, Burundi continues to depend on specialized UN agencies such as the International Bank of Reconstruction and Development (IBRD), International Monetary Fund (IMF), UN Development Program (UNDP), Food and Agriculture Organization (FAO), World Health Organization (WHO), and UN Economic and Social Committee (UNESCO) for its essential services. Burundi is a member of the Organization of African Unity (OAU), Non-Aligned Countries (NAC), French-Speaking Countries (Les pays francophones), and *la Communaute des pays des grands lacs* (CPGL).

Appendix I

Recommendations

Considering the sad events that took place in Burundi under *Front pour la democracy au Burundi* (FRODEBU) leadership, it is my opinion that FRODEBU:

1. has forfeited its right to rule the people of Burundi;

2. like Nazism, should be outlawed, as it is a genocidal political organization; and

3. leadership should be prosecuted to the fullest extent of the law even in absentia (dead or alive) for its acts committed with intent to destroy, in whole or in part, the Tutsi ethnic group in accordance with Article II (a), (b), and (c) of the United Nations (UN) Convention on the Prevention and Punishment of the Crime of Genocide. Under Article III the following acts shall be punishable:

   (a) genocide;

   (b) conspiracy to commit genocide;

   (c) direct and public incitement to commit genocide;

   (d) attempt to commit genocide; and

   (e) complicity in genocide.

Article IV states:

> Persons committing genocide or any of the other acts enumerated in Article III shall be punished, whether they are constitutionally responsible rulers, public officials or private individuals.

Under Article VI, FRODEBU leaders shall be tried by a competent tribunal where the "act of genocide was committed."

Appendix II

Brief Biographies of the Abami (Kings) of Burundi

Mwami Ntare Rushatsi Cambarantama (1550–?) was a crown prince from Buha. Mwami Cambarantama and his soldiers crossed the Muragarazi River in 1600 A.D. Armed with spears and bows and arrows, he subdued Chieftains Ruhanga, Fumbije, Jabwe, and Ruhinda. In a short period he had established himself as the uncontested *umwami* of Ibururi, Mubweru, and Ingozi. Mwami Cambarantama dispensed captured lands and cattle to his faithful followers. He is often invoked in Burundian oral history (i.e., Birenzi vya Ntare, Gira Ntare na Karyenda, Ubara Ntare ni Ruhanga, Uribesha nka Ngoma ya Ruhinda wa Gitero). Mwami Cambarantama is remembered as one of the country's best military and political strategists.

Mwami Ntare Semuganzashamba (1700-1725) came to power after a period of political stagnation and military inactivity. In an attempt to duplicate the accomplishments of Mwami Cambarantama, he attacked Rwanda and occupied the areas around Kigali, Ibufundira, and Mubugesera, and advanced north as far as Igisenyi. By the time of his death, his kingdom included Ibutare, Ibugesera, Mumugamba, and Mukumoso. He died during the battle of Butare.

Ntare Rutanganwa Rugana-Ruyenzi (Ntare the Great) (1790-1852) brought his kingdom out of fifty years of political inactivity by leading a military expedition that conquered Buyogoma, Bugufi, and Buha. In 1800 his military adventures turned toward the northeast, where he conquered Bushi and annexed the island of Idjwi (in Kivu

Lake). He attacked Rwanda and occupied its capital, Inyanza. By the time of his death most of Burundi was administered by his sons: Rwasha, Ndivyariye, Birori, and Twarereye. He is remembered as one of the most powerful leaders in Burundi history.

Mwami Mwezi Gisabo (1852-1908) inherited the throne after the death of Ntare the Great. Mwami Gisabo's older brothers refused to recognize his authority. In 1870 Mwami Gisabo's army defeated an attempted invasion by the Abajiji and Abakonikoni. This invasion originated from the eastern part of Burundi (today's Tanzania). In 1884 Mwami Gisabo's army inflicted a decisive defeat against Rumaliza (Muhammed), an Arab slave trader in the plains of Rusizi. In 1881 Catholic missionaries attempting to introduce Christianity were swiftly murdered. In 1896 Mwami Gisabo's army fought heroically against German occupation until 1903 when his army was finally defeated. He grudgingly signed the Treaty of Kiganda. Under the treaty, White Fathers expanded Catholic missions in Muyaga (1898), Mugera (1898), Buhonga (1902), Kanyinya (1904), and Rugari (1909). After the First World War, Protestant missionaries established a network of strategically located mission stations at Musema (1928), Matena (1935), Kibimba (1935), Muyebe (1935), and Kayero (1939). That was the beginning of an endless psychological conquest. In return, the German colonial administration assisted Mwami Gisabo in his efforts to defeat his principal rivals: Kilima, Maconco, Kanugunu, Busokoza, and Rusengo. Mwami Gisabo died mysteriously in 1908 after returning from a German reception in Usumbura. He was succeeded by his son, Mutaga Mbikije. Little is known of Mutaga Mbikije's brief reign. Upon his death in 1915, his younger son, Mwambutsa Bangiricenge, was crowned Mwami Mwambutsa IV. It is still a mystery why Prince Ignace Kamatari, who was more combative than his half-brother, did not succeed to the throne.

Mwami Mwambutsa IV Bangiricenge (1915-1965) was born in Mubukeye in 1915. Upon the death of Mwami Mutaga IV in 1915, Mwami Mwambutsa IV took his dynastic name (Mwambutsa). The First World War had already begun. Catholicism had established its roots in the country. The Catholic Church tried unsuccessfully to baptize the infant king. He consented to marry a newly converted young girl, Kanyonga, with whom he fathered Prince Louis Rwagasore, Princess Rose, and Princess Regina. Princess Rose married André Muhirwa, who was the *umuganwa* of Buhumuza and first Prime Minister of Burundi. Princess Regina married Umuganwa Leon Ndenzako, the first Burundian Ambassador to the United States. With the Pope's blessing, Mwami Mwambutsa IV divorced his first wife and remarried Baramparaye, with whom he fathered Mwami Ntare V (Charles Ndizeye), the last Umwami of Burundi. Throughout Mwami Mwambutsa IV's long reign he was overshadowed by the Belgian colonial administration. Policies affecting the country's economic and political development were made in Brussels without consultation with Burundian national leaders. The *umwami, abaganwa,* and *abatware* were reduced to paid colonial agents. The *umwami* played an intermediary role between the colonizer and the colonized. After the assassination of Prince Rwagasore, then Prime Minister designate, Mwami Mwambutsa IV attempted to exert power. The 1965 attempted Hutu coup frightened the aging Mwambutsa IV. He left for Switzerland with no intention to return. Heartbroken, Mwami Mwambutsa IV died in exile in Geneva (May 1977). He is remembered as a symbol of peace and unity as attested by the following song composed in 1956, his fortieth anniversary on the throne, by students of the *Ecole Normale de Kibimba* (I was a member of the choir):

> *Mwami w' Uburundi*
> *Twaje hano kugushimira ingene uganza*
> *Kungoma yawe, Burundi bwawe*
> *Bwateye imbere, bizwi hose*
> *Ganz' Usambwe,*
> *Mwami w'Uburundi we*
> *Ingoma yawe,*
> *Nihor' ihangamye*
> *Uburundi, bugukomere amashi*

Translation:

> *King of Burundi*
> *We came here to thank you for your rule*
> *During your rule, your Burundi had progressed.*
> *It is known everywhere.*
> *Rule and be respected.*
> *King of Burundi*
> *Your throne*
> *Stays strong*
> *The country should applaud.*

Mwami Ntare V (Charles Ndizeye) (24 March 1966—29 November 1966) was born in 1947 to Mwami Mwambutsa IV and Baramparaye. He attended primary school in Gitega and secondary school in Europe. He enrolled at the University of Lausanne, where he failed most of his courses. After the abortive coup of 1965, he was appointed by his absent father to coordinate the shaky government of Prime Minister Leopold Bihumugani. Still naïve, Prince Ndizeye was duped by young Tutsi "Turks" and agreed to depose his father and became Mwami Ntare V. At Rwagasore Stadium he enthusiastically declared "homme nouveaux, ère nouvelle" (a new man, a new era). "Ere nouvelle" did not last three months. In November 1966 he was overthrown by Michel Micombero, then a captain, while attending President Joseph Desiré Mobutu Sese Seko's first anniversary in Kinshasa, the Democratic Republic of the Congo (Zaire). Mwami Ntare V joined his father in exile. In 1972 he was duped again, kidnapped, and flown to Bujumbura with President Idi Amin's complicity. Mwami Ntare V was executed in Gitega on 30 April 1972. He was buried with criminals in a common grave in Nyambeho, near the Catholic Mission of Giheta. That was the end of a five-century Burundi monarchy.

Note: May the souls of Mwami Mwambutsa IV, Prince Rwagasore, and Mwami Ntare V rest in peace until their return to Mubigabiro under the guardianship of *abaterekezi*.

Appendix III

Brief Biographies of the Abaprezida
(Presidents) of Burundi

President Michel Micombero (29 November 1966—1 November 1976) was born in Murutovu into an impoverished Abahima family in 1939. He attended primary school in Rutovu and secondary school at the *College du St. Esprit* (Koleji ya Kirangakirumweru) in Bujumbura. In 1960 he was admitted to the Military Academy in Brussels. Upon his return, Mwami Mwambutsa IV appointed him Secretary of Defense of the then infant army. In 1966 Mwami Ntare V appointed him Prime Minister. Three months later he proclaimed himself President of the First Republic. He was overthrown in 1976 in a military coup and spent the rest of his life in exile in Somalia.

President Jean-Baptiste Bagaza (1976—1987) was born in Imurambi on 29 August 1946. He attended primary school at the Catholic Mission of Rutovu and secondary school at the *College du St. Esprit* (Koleji ya Kirangakirumweru). He was admitted to the *Ecole royale des cadets* in Brussels where he graduated with a degree in Military and Social Sciences. Upon his return, President Micombero appointed him *Chef d'etat major adjoint*. In 1976 Bagaza proclaimed himself President of the Second Republic. He was overthrown on 3 September 1987.

President Pierre Buyoya (1987—1993) was born in Kumutangaro, Bururi Province. He attended primary and secondary school at the Catholic Mission of Rutovu. In the early 1970s he enrolled at the

Military Academy in Brussels. When he returned, he was appointed to a series of commanding positions, including one at the prestigious Camp Muha. The military coup that ended President Bagaza's regime in 1987 selected Buyoya, then a major, for the presidency. After the Ntega-Marangara incident, and under international pressure, President Buyoya sought to balance his regime along regional and ethnic lines. He incrementally implemented a Western democratic agenda. He became a facilitator and a transitional president. He wrote a liberal Constitution, which he recently suspended. He enacted electoral laws. He created a series of commissions, organized a referendum, and legalized a multi-party system which he later banned. Political parties mushroomed along ethnic, clannish, and regional lines. President Buyoya painfully found out that he was presiding over the extermination of his own ethnic group and digging his own political grave. In the 1 June 1993 election he was overwhelmingly defeated and gracefully passed the torch to the first elected Hutu President Melchior Ndadaye. For his democratic efforts, like Gorbachev of the former Soviet Union, President Buyoya was awarded an honorarium of approximately $145,000 to set up the Foundation for Peace, Unity, and Democracy in a country where there is neither peace nor democracy. He also became an honorary member of the Western Democratic Club, and attended the Democratic Conference at the Carter Center (Atlanta, Georgia, United States) and a seminar on conflict resolution at Yale University (New Haven, Connecticut, United States). His honorarium cost Burundi dearly. His brand of democracy cost 150,000 lives. In simple arithmetic, if you divide $150,000 by 150,000 lives, his commission was one $1 per death. President Buyoya's brand of democracy also produced an attempted Tutsi genocide and a series of useless presidents: Melchior Ndadaye (three months), François Ngeze (twenty-four hours), Cyprien Ntaryamira (three months), and Sylvestre Ntibantunganya (two years). These presidents average a two-month rule. The Tutsi community at home and abroad think of President Buyoya as a spineless soldier and politically naïve. Although biologically Tutsi, his critics consider him culturally Hutu. Among the critics is his own mentor and predecessor, President Bagaza.

President Melchior Ndadaye (June 1993—October 1993) was born in Inyabihanga, Muramvya Province in 1953. He attended primary school in Kibumbu and secondary school in Kitega. During the abortive coup of 1972, he fled to Rwanda where he spent his adult life in refugee camps. He returned to Burundi under general amnesty and found a job at *Banque Meridien* in charge of credit. He was one of the founders of the FRODEBU political party, a domestic branch of *Parti pour la liberation du peuple Hutu* (PALIPEHUTU). He was elected in June 1993 and assassinated in October 1993.

President François Ngeze (21 October 1993—22 October 1993) was born in Bujumbura Province. During the abortive coup of 1972 he fled to Rwanda where he spent his adult life in refugee camps. He returned to Burundi under refugee amnesty and taught in schools. President Buyoya appointed him governor of Bujumbura and soon thereafter, Interior Minister. He was elected to the National Assembly in 1993. During the abortive coup in October 1993, he was appointed President of the Republic, a position that lasted twenty-four hours. He was shortly arrested and imprisoned.

President Cyprien Ntaryamira (January 1994—April 1994) was born in Mubimbi, Bujumbura Province. During the abortive coup of 1972 he fled to Rwanda where he spent his adult life in refugee camps. He returned to Burundi under refugee amnesty. After the elections of 1993, he was appointed Minister of Agriculture. Upon President Ndadaye's assassination he was appointed interim president. He was killed with President Juvenal Havyarimana of Rwanda in a mysterious airplane crash on 6 April 1994.

President Sylvestre Ntibantunganya (June 1994—25 July 1996) was born in Igishubi, Kitega Province. During the 1972 abortive coup he fled to Rwanda where he spent most of his adult life in refugee camps. He returned to Burundi under refugee amnesty and was one of the founders of FRODEBU. After the 1993 elections, Ntibantunganya was appointed Foreign Minister. Upon President Ndadaye's assassination he became the Speaker of the Parliament. After the death of President Ntaryamira, Ntibantunganya inherited the presidency. President Ntibantunganya was overthrown in a military coup on 25 July 1996.

President Pierre Buyoya (25 July 1996–)

Appendix IV

Circa 1500   Mwami Ntare Rushatsi Cambarantama establishes Burundi.

1700–1725   Mwami Ntare Semuganzashamba conquers Rwanda, Bufundu, and Bugesera.

1790–1852   Mwami Ntare Rutanganwa Ruganda-Ruyenzi (Ntare the Great) conquers Bushi, Bugufi, Buyogoma, and Idjwi (an island in Lake Kivu).

1852–1908   Mwami Mwezi Gisabo defeats Rumaliza (Muhammed), an Arab slave trader. Catholic missionaries are murdered. German occupation. Introduction of Christianity.

1914–1940   The First World War. Burundi becomes part of a League of Nations mandate under a Belgian administration. Introduction of European economy and education. Crown Prince Bangiricenge is crowned Mwami Mwambutsa IV.

1940-1960   The Second World War. Burundi is converted into a United Nations (UN) trusteeship under a Belgian administration. Prince Louis Rwagasore creates *Union et progres nationale* (UPRONA).

1960–1970   The UN supervises elections. An UPRONA victory. Prince Rwagasore is designated Prime Minister. Prince Rwagasore is assassinated. Burundi becomes independent. Umuganwa Ntidendereza and his younger brother, Joseph Birori, are hung in Gitega. Prince Ignace Kamatari and Prime Minister Ngendandumwe are assassinated. An attempted coup and the execution of culprits. Tutsi massacre in Muramvya Province. Mwami Mwambutsa IV is deposed. Crown Prince Charles Ndizeye is crowned Mwami Ntare V. Monarchy is abolished. President Michel Micombero proclaims the First Republic of Burundi.

1970–1980   Inter-ethnic civil war. President Micombero is deposed. President Jean-Baptiste Bagaza proclaims the Second Republic of Burundi.

1980–1990   President Bagaza is deposed. President Pierre Buyoya proclaims the Third Republic of Burundi. Ntega-Marangara inter-ethnic strife.

1990–   Hutu attacks in Kayanza, Cibitoke, Bubanza, and Bujumbura. Presidential elections. President Buyoya is defeated. An attempted coup on 3 July 1993. Melchior Ndadaye becomes President. President Ndadaye is assassinated. François Ngeze becomes the president for a day. Inter-ethnic civil war. Attempted Tutsi genocide. Interim President Cyprien Ntaryamira is killed in a mysterious plane crash with President Juvenal Havyarimana of Rwanda. Sylvestre Ntibantunganya is selected as the next president. Kamenge incidents. Prime Minister Anatole Kanyenkiko resigns under UPRONA pressure. Leonard Nyangoma declares "Hutu War" against the government. Hutu attacks in Bugendana and Mucibitoke. President Ntibantunganya is overthrown. The end of *Front pour la democracy au Burundi* (FRODEBU) rule. President Buyoya is appointed for the second time.

Appendix V

Selected Important Dates in African History

800–586 B.C.   Carthage becomes an important commercial center.

750 B.C.   The Kushite Kingdom of Sudan becomes an important trading partner with Rome and India.

500 B.C.   The Kingdom of Axum (Ethiopia) becomes an important trading partner with the Near East and India.

149–146 B.C.   Rome conquers Carthage.

300–320 A.D.   Christianity is introduced in the Kingdom of Axum.

439 A.D.   Carthage becomes the capital of the Kingdom of Vandal.

698 A.D.   Carthage is conquered by the Saracene ending Byzantine rule.

700 A.D.   Arabs conquer North Africa. Ghana becomes a major empire. Timbuktu becomes an important trading and cultural center.

800 A.D.   Arabs colonize Madagascar and Zanzibar. Arab slave trade.

990 A.D.   The Zimbabwe civilization flourishes.

1324 A.D.	King Mansa Musa's pilgrimage to Mecca.
1350	Benin becomes an important trading center. Agreement with the Kingdom of Portugal.
1400	The Kingdom of Baruba conquers Katanga and Kivu.
1415–1491	Portugal explores African coast. Trade with Portugal. Colonization of Mozambique.
1529	Ethiopian-Somali War. Portuguese intervention. Somalia is defeated.
1562	Sir John Hawkins of England establishes slave trade between Africa and America.
1652	Holland establishes colonies in Capetown.
1680	German colonization of certain parts of Africa and America.
1787	Great Britain establishes a colony in Freetown, Sierra Leone.
1799	European powers (Portugal, Holland, France, Spain, Denmark, and Sweden) establish slave trade posts along West African coasts.
1806–1807	England annexes Cape Province. Slave trade outlawed.
1822	Liberia is founded by freed American slaves and gains independence in 1847.
1830	France conquers Algeria.
1835	Boers trek and establish the Republics of Transvaal, Natal, and the Orange Free State.

1841	David Livingstone explores Central Africa and the Lake Tanganyika area.
1874–1889	Stanley explores the Congo River and meets Livingstone in Kigoma.
1878	Zulu revolt against British colonial rule.
1884–1885	The Berlin Conference and scramble for Africa.
1889	Emperor Menelik of Ethiopia signs a treaty with Italy.
1908	Recognition of French, Spanish, and German interests in Morocco.
1910	Establishment of the Union of South Africa (Cape of Good Hope, Natal, the Orange Free State, and Transvaal).
1914–1918	The First World War. Defeat of Germany. League of Nations.
1930–1936	Haile Selassie is crowned Emperor of Ethiopia. Italy invades Ethiopia. British intervention and the defeat of the Italian army.
1939–1945	The Second World War. Axis powers defeated. Establishment of trusteeship territories.
1952	Mau-Mau rebellion in Kenya. End of monarchy in Egypt.
1955–1959	African nationalism. Bandung Conference. Ghana and Guinea become independent.
1960–1970	Most of African countries gain independence. Creation of the Organization of African Unity (OAU). Civil war in Congo (Leopoldville) and Sudan. Tutsi genocide in Rwanda. Prince Louis

Rwagasore and Prime Minister Patrice Lumumba are assassinated. Mwami Mwambutsa IV and Mwami Ntare V are deposed. United Nations (UN) Secretary-General Dag Hammarskjold is killed in a plane crash. Katanga and Biafra secedes. Civil war in Nigeria. Unilateral Declaration of Independence (UDI) in Rhodesia. Kwame Nkrumah is overthrown. Wars of liberation in Angola, Guinea Bissau, Mozambique, Namibia, and Zimbabwe. Violent protests against apartheid in South Africa.

1970–1980   Collapse of Portuguese empire in Africa. Emperor Haile Selassie is overthrown. Inter-ethnic civil war in Burundi. Civil war in Angola and Sudan. Ethiopia and Somalia war over Ogaden. United States President Jimmy Carter visits Nigeria and Liberia (the first United States President to visit Africa).

1980–1990   Nelson Mandela is released from prison. Civil war in Angola, Mozambique, Chad, Sudan, and Liberia. Coups and counter-coups occur in most African states.

1990–   Elections in Burundi. President Ndadaye is assassinated in Burundi. Attempted Tutsi genocide in Burundi. President Juvenal Havyarimana is assassinated in Rwanda. Tutsi genocide in Rwanda. Mandela is elected President of South Africa. UN International Tribunal on Rwanda in Arusha. Hutu-Tutsi civil war in Burundi. *Coup d'état* and re-appointment of former President Buyoya to the presidency.

3

THE CONGO REBELLION

THE ROOT OF REBELLION IN THE CONGO (ZAIRE)

President Joseph Desiré Mobutu Sese Seko,[66] son of an ethnic
Ngbandi hotel maid, was born on 14 October 1930 in Lisala, Equator
Province. Here he attended local Catholic schools before enrolling in
the Belgian colonial army. During the movement for independence,
a young Mobutu joined Patrice Lumumba's *Mouvement nationale
Congolais* (MNC). He became Lumumba's private secretary. In
1959 Mobutu accompanied Lumumba to the *Table ronde* in Brussels
to determine Congo's independence. Upon becoming Prime Minister
in 1960, Lumumba appointed his young protégé Secretary of State
for National Defense and Chief of the Army Staff. A year later, the
ungrateful Mobutu conspired in the arrest and ultimate assassination
of Prime Minister Lumumba with the assistance of the United States
Central Intelligence Agency (CIA).

After a period of indecision (what a United States journalist called
a Black Hamlet), Mobutu seized power in a bloodless coup on 24
November 1965. He accused Prime Minister Kimba and four other
cabinet ministers of treason. They were publicly hung. President
Mobutu established himself as an uncontested autocrat. Katanga and
Kassai attempted to secede but failed. The Simba rebellion had been
defeated. The leaders of independence—Lumumba, Tshombe, and
Kasavubu—were already dead. Mulopwe Albert Kalonji of Kassai
had been reduced to a business peddler.

President Mobutu proceeded to consolidate his autocratic power
through ruse and cunning. To outsiders President Mobutu seemed to
be a symbol of order and stability in a sea of chaos. The constitution
he crafted gave him unlimited power. His work became a law in itself.

74

In the early 1970s, he decreed the ideology of authenticity. Zairians were forced to abandon their Christian baptismal names and European dress. Authentic men wore tunics; authentic women wore wraps made of African prints. Coincidentally, President Mobutu's relatives owned the authentic garment industry.

Le Guide, as President Mobutu liked to call himself, was often depicted on state television as a superhero descending from the heavens. In times of troubles he consulted African spiritual advisors who claimed to have magical powers and who often told him to shed the blood of his enemies in order to revive himself.

By rephrasing Lumumba's statement, "The Congo made me and I will make the Congo," President Mobutu declared, "There was no Zaire before me and there will be no Zaire after me either." His prediction proved to be right. Soon after his fall, Zaire became the Democratic Republic of the Congo.

Under the aegis of "Zairianization" in the early 1970s, President Mobutu created bogus companies through which he secreted $300 million. He is reported to have misappropriated $1 billion of aid from the United States. In another case he split $400 million in commissions on copper revenues with his senior advisors. By the end of his rule, President Mobutu controlled approximately one-third of the nation's revenues. He had become one of the world's richest men. Like King Leopold's Congo Free State,[67] President Mobutu treated Zaire as if it was his own property. Under President Mobutu's rule, theft became an acceptable, institutionalized way of life.

President Mobutu's cardinal rules were simple: Those who make their fortunes in high offices should not condemn others and ill-gotten gains must be generously shared with the chief. An opposition leader commented, "Our disease started at the top. Mobutu has stolen more money than anyone."

President Mobutu's system of pauperizing drove Zairian people into abject poverty. An observer commented on President Mobutu's military attitude, "We are going to eat you like monkey meat.[68] They knew no pity for us."

Doctors ignored poor patients. Factory workers stole parts to sell. College graduates became peddlers. Ordinary workers survived by bartering their meager possessions. Rubber, coffee, and banana plantations reverted to bush. Corruption began to choke businesses.

Inflation climbed to a four-digit annual rate, eroding the purchasing power of an average worker.

After sixty-five years of harsh Belgian colonial rule and forty-four years of President Mobutu's mismanagement, Zaire, a country endowed with natural resources,[69] became one of the poorest in Africa.

The Rwanda Connection

Unlike the 1960s Simba rebellion, the 1996 rebellion in the Democratic Republic of the Congo (Zaire) has its roots in the 1994 Rwandan Tutsi genocide. After three months of inter-ethnic civil war in Rwanda, more than one million ethnic Hutu, including former military personnel, militia (Interahamwe), and civil servants, found themselves in the Democratic Republic of the Congo's (Zaire) refugee camps. Hutu insurgents conducted sporadic raids inside Rwanda and Burundi and stirred inter-ethnic hatred within the Democratic Republic of the Congo's (Zaire) local population.

To add insult to injury, in October 1996 the governor of South Kivu threatened to expel ethnic Tutsi-Banyamulenge (Abatutsi b'Abanyamulenge) from the area that was once a part of Rwanda before its annexation to the Belgian Congo. The Tutsi-Banyamulenge are ethnically related to Rwandan Tutsis. Their territory in the eastern section of the Democratic Republic of the Congo (Zaire) was once a part of traditional Rwanda. It was annexed to the Belgian Congo in 1910. The threat triggered an armed Tutsi rebellion. Rwanda, Uganda, and Burundi provided covert logistical support, in part to punish Mobutu for harboring Hutu insurgents.

The Tutsi Offensive

On 13 October 1996, Tutsi guerrillas under *Alliance des forces démocratiques pour la liberation du Congo* attacked the Zairian government's military positions. Laurent Kabila's rebel forces were estimated to consist of seventy thousand men. The *Alliance* was backed by Angola, Burundi, Rwanda, Uganda, and Zambia. They captured the strategic towns of Uvira, Bukavu, and Goma. Hutu refugee camps were permanently closed, forcing thousands of refugees to return to Rwanda or flee westward into the jungles of the Democratic Republic of the Congo (Zaire). Rebel commander Kabila[70] announced, "We have fulfilled the will of the international community." Then the Rwandan Tutsi-dominated government called on the UN to redesign its mission.

What began as a localized Tutsi uprising became a multi-ethnic, anti-Mobutu movement under the *Alliance des forces democratiques pour la liberation du Congo*. The *Alliance* included the famous Mai-Mai insurgents. Kabila declared, "We are fighting to put an end to this useless state that no longer exists."[71]

Mobutu prepared for his counter-offensive. From the French Riviera, where he was convalescing from prostate cancer surgery, he issued this statement:

> If it is Zairians who are attacking Zaire, they will be treated as such. If they are invaders, we will deal with them. We will return their trouble all the way back to Rwanda.[72]

The Tutsi were systematically murdered in Kivu Province. Ethnic Tutsi were hunted, dragged from their houses, beaten, and, in most cases, murdered in Kinshasa. Tutsi women were repeatedly raped. Zairians marching in solidarity with Hutu hoodlums shouted at Prime Minister Kengo Wa Dongo:[73]

> *Of Tutsi origin, Kengo must go*
> *The people have vomited Kengo and Tutsi*
> *The Tutsi have revealed their true face*
> *Their women are unnaturally fertile*
> *They want to own everything*
> *They are trying to take over Zairian land as well.*[74]

Immigration agents searched Tutsi homes and seized their travel documents. The government hired a band of three hundred Serbian mercenaries, many of whom were veterans of Bosnia's genocidal war. Mobutu ordered the re-armament of the former Rwandan army. According to military analysts, the Zairian army, which consisted of one million men, was a collection of undisciplined rival groups whose main mission was to protect Mobutu. Most of its commanders were recruited from Mobutu's homeland, Equator Province.

The rebels were not scared. They captured town after town. The strategic town of Kindu, defended by Rwandan troops, fell to the rebels. In March 1997, Kisangani (Stanleyville), defended by Serbian mercenaries, also fell. This was a cause of embarrassment for Mobutu.

Serbian mercenaries blew up an ammunitions depot and fled. Undisciplined and demoralized, Zairian troops fled while looting, chanting, "We won't die for one hundred thousand zaires a month."

Zaire's rubber-stamp parliament flexed its muscles and voted to impeach Prime Minister Dongo instead of the "absentee landlord." Upon his return from Europe, Mobutu accepted Prime Minister Dongo's resignation and appointed opposition leader Etienne Tshisekedi to the position of prime minister in an attempt to defuse the situation. In a dramatic move, Tshisekedi moved to dissolve the parliament and excluded Mobutu's allies from the government.

One commentator compared Mobutu to a dying lion hunted by hyenas, "We don't want Mobutu to die. We want the man who debased us to live to see himself overthrown." Another citizen commented, "It does not matter if they are Tutsi. They came here to liberate us . . . . We will treat them as friends. They are liberators."

In Kisangani the crowd cheered rebel commander Kabila:

> Long live the Liberator Kabila
> Welcome Papa Kabila
> Chirac's son (Mobutu) is dead
> We are free.

On 4 April 1997 rebel forces captured Mbuji-Mayi, a major diamond mining center encircling Lubumbashi (Elizabethville). In Shaba (Katanga) deserting soldiers from the Twenty-First Brigade declared common cause with the rebels and voted to fight government forces. Kabila seized a government-owned industrial diamond mining company in Mbuji-Mayi and signed a multimillion dollar contract with a United States corporation to mine zinc in Kapushi and cobalt in Kilowezi. A Belgian company expressed interest in the exploitation of gold in Kilo-Moto and a Canadian company paid fifty million dollars to mine copper and cobalt in Shaba (Katanga). Investment bankers from the United States flew to Lubumbashi (Elizabethville) to negotiate with rebel leaders.

In Kinshasa thousands of student protesters confronted Mobutu's armored vehicles, a reminder of the 1989 Tianenmen Square student uprising in Beijing, China. The rebel commander vowed to march to Kinshasa.

ETHNIC IRREDENTISM VS. INTERNATIONAL CONSPIRACY

Ethnic Irredentism

From the outset, Hutu theorists blamed President Yoweri Museveni[75] of Uganda for having a secret agenda to recreate a Tutsi empire in the Great Lakes region.[76] However, Uganda did not have the military power or economic resources for such a grandiose enterprise.

Regardless, regional leaders began to believe the Hutu theory. The Hutu ethnic theory was based in part in the connection between Ankole, Buha, Burundi, and Rwanda. These territories were organized simultaneously in 1500 A.D. along Lakes Edward, Albert, Kivu, Mweru, and Cohoha. During the colonial era Burundi and Rwanda retained their original entities although they each lost some lands. Ankole became incorporated into the British Protectorate of Uganda. Buha was incorporated in the British Tanganyika Trust Territory (Tanzania). Colonial boundaries changed little because of traditional Tutsi interaction. In fact, European education and modernized means of transportation facilitated communication.

President Arap Moi called for a comprehensive investigation of President Museveni. Furthermore, he refused to hand over the Hutu criminals indicted by the UN International Tribunal for Rwanda. The Tanzanian government recommended an economic embargo to debilitate Burundi. It surrendered its embassy to Hutu rebels. Participating regional countries included Ethiopia, Kenya, Rwanda, Uganda, the Democratic Republic of the Congo (Zaire), and Zambia. The embargo was lifted in April 1997 at the Arusha regional meeting. Mobutu's government continued to harbor Hutu insurgents from Rwanda and Burundi.

International Conspiracy

Since the 1898 Fashoda incident,[77] Anglo-French rivalry in Africa has not ceased. France attempted to fill the economic and political vacuum left by Belgium in the Democratic Republic of the Congo (Zaire). Rwanda and Burundi have been consistently checked by the Anglo-Saxon bloc. After the French-trained Rwandan Hutu army was defeated by an Anglo-Saxonized Ugandan Tutsi army in 1994, France was reminded of its humiliation at Fashoda.

Disappointed by the 1994 failure of Operation Turquoise in Rwanda, France attempted a comeback by proposing to the UN Security Council an immediate humanitarian intervention in the eastern section of the Democratic Republic of the Congo (Zaire) with five thousand troops. UN Secretary-General Boutros Boutros-Ghali wrote to the UN Security Council, "We are confronted by a new Genocide. I call it 'Genocide by starvation'."

The French proposal was mocked by a United States department spokesman, "The cowboys just blowing into town is not going to solve the problem."

Rwanda's Tutsi-dominated government announced that it would block international relief efforts if France was involved.

South African Vice President Mbeki cautioned that the rescue mission may destabilize the region, "Sending troops to Zaire without considering comprehensive answers for the tensions that exist in the region will prove to be no solution at all."

France and Belgium were ruled out as negative influences in the region. Again, the move was considered an Anglo-Saxon coup. As a compromise, the Clinton Administration approved an international rescue mission for the Democratic Republic of the Congo (Zaire) led by Canada[78] with mandates:

Open airfields in Bukavu and Goma

Secure three mile corridors from Rwanda and Uganda
  into the Democratic Republic of the Congo (Zaire)

Protect international aid workers

Protect and encourage Hutu refugees to return to Rwanda

Although the mission was finally abandoned, the crisis in the Democratic Republic of the Congo (Zaire) had been managed largely by the Anglo-Saxon bloc. Kabila's rebel forces pre-empted the international conspiracy by permanently closing refugee camps along the border of Rwanda.

The Democratic Republic of the Congo's (Zaire) refugee camps were filled past capacity: Mugunga Camp had 400,000 Hutu refugees (40,000 were former Rwandan Hutu soldiers and 10,000 Interahamwe); Goma Refugee Camp had 300,000 Hutu refugees;

Bukavu Refugee Camp had 500,000 Hutu refugees; and Uvira Refugee Camp had 500,000 refugees (143,000 were from Burundi). There were 80,000 Hutu refugees near Kisangani (55,000 in Kasese and 30,000 in Biaro). Many of the refugees suffered from cholera, malaria, diarrhea, and hunger. Some refugees went on night raids to steal food and clothes from nearby farmers. A conflict between the local population and Zairian rebels prompted the United Nations Secretary-General Kofi Annan to accuse Laurent Kabila's forces of waging a campaign of slow extermination. Other international commentators spoke of a campaign of "retaliatory genocide" or "final solution." One and a half million Hutu refugees in Tanzania returned to Rwanda.

In May 1997 about 50,000 Hutu refugees, some of whom were former Hutu soldiers and militia, trekked toward Congo (Brazzaville), near the town of Mbandanaka on the eastern bank of the Congo River. Five thousand refugees were flown back to Rwanda. Three thousand crossed the Congo river to Liranga, Congo/Brazzaville. They suffered from exhaustion, malnutrition, and malaria. Most, if not all, were in need of food, shelter, and medicine. The United Nations High Commission on Refugees (UNHCR) estimates that fifty thousand Hutu refugees were killed by Zairian rebels and forty thousand were trapped along the Congo River. Untold numbers died during the long walk through Zairian jungles. Thousands of ethnic Tutsi were killed and the rest fled to Rwanda.

Initial recruits included mostly ethnic Tutsi (Abatutsi) guerrilla fighters who had fought with Yoweri Museveni against President Milton Obote of Uganda in the 1980s and with General Paul Kagame's in Rwanda's civil war. The objective was to clean up the Hutu refugee camps along Rwanda's border. Revenge was also one of the most important factors. As United States President Thomas Jefferson once wrote, "The tree of liberty must be refreshed from time to time with blood of patriots."

Likewise, the Tutsi blood of patriots had to be shed. Mukala Kadima-Mzuji depicts the spiral of war and chaos in Zaire in his poetry:

Gorged with blood
From thousands of innocent souls
Lying silently and emotionless
On clods of scorched earth.

As the rebels had no mechanized divisions, artillery, aircraft, engineers, modern means of communication, or diplomatic relationships, neighboring countries played crucial roles. The Ugandian government provided artillery and armored carriers. Rwanda and Burundi contributed troops, advisers, and equipment. The government of Jose Eduardo dos Santos in Angola contributed money, training, commandos, tanks, airlift, and heavy equipment. In the final phase of the seven-month conflict, Angolan troops participated in the battle in Kenge. The governments of Tanzania, Zambia, and Zimbabwe joined the anti-Mobutu diplomatic crusade, in part to punish him for his role in the destabilization in the region.

THE REBEL OFFENSIVE

Alliance des forces democratiques pour la liberation du Congo attacked Hutu refugee camps, dispersing more than one million Hutu refugees. The *Alliance* attracted ethnic Nande, Hunde, Ngilima, and Mai-Mai. Katangese guards joined Laurent Desiré Kabila's movement. In December 1996, rebels, with the help of Ugandan soldiers, seized Bunia, Butembo, Beni, and Watsa. As the war progressed, deserters of President Mobutu's army joined the rebels.

Kabila ingeniously balanced various ethnic groups and regional power blocs. One of the rebel soldiers explained, "We are an alliance. We have all kinds of people among us. We are Africans. We are Congolese." Kabila vowed to oust Mobutu, "We are fighting to put an end to this useless state that no longer exists."

The rebels' strategy and tactics were similar to that of General Kagame in Rwanda's civil war. Motivation and discipline were essential. The identity of senior commanders remained anonymous. Rebels attacked from different directions leaving an opening for President Mobutu's soldiers to escape. Government soldiers who surrendered or were captured were treated humanely. The cost in terms of lives, ammunitions, and property damages was minimized. The war was transformed into an anti-Mobutu referendum. A government military colonel commented, "The war is no longer a military problem. Elsewhere we go, the population is with the rebels."

Preceded by a network of spies who spread rumors and planted tracts, the rebels marched confidently from victory to victory. More troops were recruited as the war progressed. An observer commented, "Mobutu has tricked us all until now. The mystification is over. It is the end of Mobutu's magic. The time has finally come for him to go."

Supporters of Etienne Tshisekedi declared Kinshasa "dead." One opposition leader commented, "Today we have a dead city, dead villages, dead schools, and a dead country. What we are waiting for is a dead Mobutu."

From Goma, the rebel's headquarters, Kabila sent a three-day ultimatum to President Mobutu, "I am waiting for Mobutu to make a decision for his departure."

The momentum continued unchecked. The rebels captured Llebo, Tshikapa, Doweto, Kikwit, Lisala, Matadi, and Mbanza-Ngungu, thus penetrating Bas-Zaire. In May 1997 they captured Kenge, Bundundu, and Bandaka. United States Ambassador to Zaire Daniel H. Simpson called on General Likulia Bolongo to order his remaining troops to allow the rebels to enter Kinshasa peacefully. A history professor at the University of Kinshasa commented, "If President Mobutu decides to give up power, there will be no fighting. That way there will be no looting or loss of lives."

On 17 May 1997 the rebels captured a military base near Ndjili International Airport and infiltrated the center of Kinshasa. Panicked, President Mobutu's forces fought among themselves. Some surrendered while others fled looting. Then the population welcomed the rebels chanting, "Mobutu is a devil. Congo, we are free."

PRESIDENT MOBUTU'S COUNTER-OFFENSIVE

On the Domestic Front

Pro-Mobutu elements attacked ethnic Tutsi. An observer commented, "I was lucky that my wife and daughter were staying elsewhere. They were raping girls as young as ten and twelve, forcing their fathers to watch." In Kinshasa, immigration agents searched Tutsi homes and seized their travel documents.

As soon as President Mobutu returned from Europe, Prime Minister Dongo submitted his resignation and left immediately for Switzerland. He was later accused of raiding the treasury, siphoning off tax revenues, and trafficking in currency.

After the fall of Lubumbashi, President Mobutu reacted desperately by dismissing the newly appointed Prime Minister Tshisekedi, declaring a state of emergency, and appointing a military government headed by General Bolongo. An opposition leader commented, "There is no way of turning the clock back. Mobutu's rule is finished. If he does not understand we will bring Kabila here to explain to him."

Upon the capture of Bandaka, President Mobutu's government responded by imposing a curfew and calling on the population to defend the capital.

On the International Front

President Mobutu sought intervention from France, Morocco, and Israel. He tried to recruit mercenaries from "Executive Outcomes." As the price proved prohibitive, he turned to Serbian mercenaries, some of whom were notorious veterans of Bosnia's genocidal war. Flying MIG-24 combat gunships, Serbian and French mercenaries indiscriminately bombed civilian targets in Bukavu, Walikale, and Shabunda. Their deranged commander Colonel Dominic (Yugo) had a reputation of executing, beating, electrocuting, and slashing the throats of suspects for minor offenses.

At the peace conference brokered by South African President Nelson Mandela, President Mobutu agreed to transfer power to a transitional authority provided that Kabila agree to a cessation of hostilities and establishment of a consensus government. Instead, Kabila demanded President Mobutu's peaceful surrender. As both positions became increasingly irreconcilable, the peace talks ended inconclusively. Kabila told reporters:

> Mobutu has asked me to give him eight days while he considers our demand to resign. If Mobutu surrenders power now, I will guarantee his safety and that of his biological family. If not, we will have to chase him away in humiliation.

At a Francophone summit in Libreville (Gabon), France tried to smooth President Mobutu's exit with dignity. But Mobutu entertained the idea of remaining interim president until a successor was elected, and if incapacitated, allowing the power to revert to the president of the National Assembly, Archbishop Laurent Monsengwo. Kabila rejected Mobutu's proposals and refused to attend the second round of peace talks. Instead he flew to Capetown (South Africa) to meet privately with President Mandela.

As the second round of peace talks collapsed, one of Mobutu's military commanders commented, "The government knows that Mobutu must leave now. If he attempts to return home, his plane would be prevented from landing or would be shot down." A member of the National Assembly commented, "Mobutu is hard-headed. A man who looks after himself. He abandoned Zaire a long time ago." An observer commented, "Lord Jesus, please save us. It is always the people who suffer the most. Just let us survive these next days."

The unexpected defiant return of Mobutu to Kinshasa from a second round of failed peace talks brokered by President Mandela off Pointe-Noire (Congo) triggered a resolute revolt from the army. A diplomat commented, "The government troops are abandoning their vehicles and equipment as the rebels approach."

Mobutu's close associates also panicked and fled to neighboring Congo (Brazzaville) by ferry. One of Mobutu's security guards commented, "If I have to open fire on someone, I will. This is no time to fuss over immigration checks."

THE COLLAPSE OF PRESIDENT MOBUTU'S COUNTER-OFFENSIVE

General Bolongo, accompanied by the Defense Minister and Army Chief of Staff General Mahele Lieko Bukungo, and the Commander of the Special Presidential Division General Nzimbi Ngbale, confronted Mobutu with military realities and told him to leave, "We can't defend the city. We can't protect you. Therefore, you should go."

During a heated argument, General Bukungo stood up, left the room, and slammed the door—a gesture that would cost him his life. At the third round of meetings, Mobutu agreed to leave and formally handed over the power to General Bolongo. Afterwards, General Bolongo's spokesman commented, "We are no longer occupying ourselves with military matters. The only thing left is politics."

Mobutu's last act as Chief of State was to officially cremate the embalmed body of Juvenal Havyarimana, the former president of Rwanda. He had kept Havyarimana's body in his village, Gbadolite, for three years. A security guard who was in charge of the corpse commented, "If it were up to me I would have dumped it into the river."

The next day, Mobutu, his wife, a concubine (the twin sister of his wife), and three children left the capital, flew to Gbadolite, and then to Lome (Togo) to exile in either Morocco or France.

Mobutu's departure was not the end of the drama itself. Loyalists (including his own son, Captain Kongulu) vowed to fight to the end, and if necessary, to assassinate any army commanders who preferred negotiations with Kabila's rebels. As Army Chief of Staff General Bukungo tried to calm the situation in Tshatshi Camp, loyalists accused him of being a traitor and shot him at point-blank range in the head. General Bolongo escaped into the French Embassy and later fled to Congo(Brazzaville). General Ngbale (Mobutu's nephew) also escaped to Congo/ Brazzaville, as did Mobutu's son, Captain Kongulu.

French Fashoda Syndrome

As Kabila's rebel forces advanced from victory to victory, France's effort to remain the patron of ex-Belgian colonies resumed. Through Geolink (a Paris-based telecommunications company), the French government conducted covert operations, recruited three hundred French and Serbian mercenaries, and supplied arms to Mobutu's government. But French efforts to revive a dead army were doomed from the beginning. Anti-Mobutu sentiment in Zaire grew. One of Mobutu's generals commented, "When a fish is rotten, all the seasoning can't make it edible."

Another military analyst compared Mobutu's army to a "house eaten by termites." As in the case of Rwanda and Burundi, France continued to support Mobutu to the end. Suspecting an Anglo-Saxon role in President Mandela's brokered peace talks, the French government convened its own mini-summit in Libreville, Gabon. France asked the United States to pressure Kabila into stopping further military advances. Instead, the Clinton Administration told France to tell Mobutu to get out. The French Embassy in Kinshasa shredded or burned confidential documents relating to her relations with Mobutu. The defeat of Mobutu's French-trained army in the hands of an Anglo-Saxonized rebels again reminded France of the Fashoda syndrome.

Anglo-Saxon Hegemony

Since the United States CIA assisted in his 1965 coup, Mobutu had been a willing instrument of United States' sponsored policies in central Africa. United States President George Bush once referred to him as the United States' oldest and most valuable friend on the African continent. But with the end of the Cold War, Mobutu (like the Shah of Iran, President Noriega of Panama, and President Douvalier of Haiti) had outlived his usefulness to United States geo-political interests. A State Department spokesman commented, "Mobutuism is in a state of disrepair. The end of Mobutu's autocratic regime is inevitable." The United States House of Representatives International Relations Committee called on Mobutu, ". . . to resign immediately and leave the country." In a letter to Mobutu, United States President William Jefferson Clinton demanded immediate face-to-face discussions with Kabila and immediate withdrawal from the political scene.

When Mobutu asked President Clinton's special envoy Ambassador Bill Richardson why, after many years of loyal service, he has been abandoned, Richardson answered him frankly, "The mess you are in is not our mess. You did not govern your own country."

Off Pointe-Noire (Congo), on the South African naval ship Outeniqua, peace talks were brokered by the United States and South Africa. Ambassador Richardson insisted on the need to ease Mobutu out of power and Kabila to enter Kinshasa peacefully,[79] "A soft landing would avoid violence and chaos."[80]

A diplomatic observer commented:

> The decision for Mobutu to leave has been made. The only question is whether Mobutu will jump into a helicopter to flee Kinshasa in time or not. And whether Kabila will seize undivided power, or will be persuaded to share it with other political forces.

As soon as Mobutu's regime collapsed, the Clinton Administration recognized Kabila's government and pledged to help him build an "inclusive" democracy.

The Aftermath

With the stroke of a pen, Kabila suspended Zaire's constitution, promised a government of national salvation, created a constituent assembly, and declared himself President of the Democratic Republic of the Congo (reverting to a name used at the time of Independence in 1960). The Voice of Zaire was renamed the Voice of Congo. The national radio played the "Independence Cha Cha," a popular song at the time of Independence. In Kinshasa, President Kabila's forces manned key positions and called on Mobutu's soldiers to surrender, "Government soldiers were given until 10:00 A.M. today to surrender weapons and report to any of the military camps around Kinshasa."

Many soldiers surrendered their weapons at Tshatshi Camp. The military governor of Kinshasa also surrendered. As President Kabila triumphantly entered Kinshasa on 20 May 1997, a jubilant population waved banners that read, "Long live the Congo!" A young woman standing by claimed, "I am a Congolese. This is our history." Another commented, "We had suffered for thirty-two years. These soldiers are Congolese, not Zairians. We are proud of them." Still another commented, "In three decades, Mobutu formed an army of thieves. Today we are doing little bit cleaning up." Anti-French sentiment was heard throughout the streets, "The French have always wanted to be our masters and have Africans as their slaves."

Appendix I

October–December 1996

The governor of South Kivu Province announces the government's intention to expel ethnic Tutsi-Banyamulenge (Abatutsi b'Abanyamulenge). The warning triggered a rebellion. The Tutsi-Banyamulenge captured the town of Uvira (northern shore of Lake Tanganyika), then Bukavu and Goma. The Rwandan Hutu refugee camp at Mugunga was overrun. Approximately seven hundred thousand Hutu refugees returned to Rwanda. The rest fled westward deep into the Democratic Republic of the Congo's (Zaire) jungle. The United Nations' (UN) multinational intervention plan was abandoned.

January–March 1997

President Joseph Desiré Mobutu Sese Seko's government prepares its counter-offensive. His hired Serbian mercenaries began to bomb the towns of Bukavu, Shabunda, and Walikale to no avail. The strategic towns of Kisangani and Kindu fall to the rebels. The UN proposes a five-point cease-fire plan. The fall of Kisangani.

April–May 1997

Mediation efforts in South Africa. The fall of Lubumbashi (Elizabethville). Appointment and dismissal of Prime Minister Etienne Tshisekedi. Demonstrations in Kinshasa. President Mobutu declares a state of emergency and appoints General Likulia Bolongo, a French-trained lawyer, as the head of the military government.

Rebels capture Llebo, Tshikapa, Doweto, Kikwit (a major town east of Kinshasa), Lisala (Mobutu's birthplace), Mbanza-Ngungu (capital of Bas-Zaire), and Matadi (a port city). Diplomatic negotiations take place aboard South African naval ship Outeniqua off Pointe-Noire, Congo. The talks are brokered by South African President Nelson Mandela and United States Ambassador to the UN Bill Richardson. A Francophone conference is held in Libreville, Gabon. A second round of talks collapses because Laurent Kabila refuses to attend. President Mobutu returns to the Democratic Republic of the Congo (Zaire) for the last time. On 16 May 1997 Mobutu leaves the country for Togo. Kabila suspends Zaire's constitution and declares himself President of the Democratic Republic of the Congo. Mobutu's army surrenders. The *Alliance des forces democratiques pour la liberation du Congo* enters Kinshasa. President Kabila arrives in the capital from Lubumbashi.

2

Genocide From Global Perspectives

*Genocide recognizes neither geographic boundaries
nor ethnic monopolies. It has become an
incurable man-made disease.*

4

Europe, Asia, the Americas, and Africa

Europe

European history has recorded numerous incidences of genocidal activity. During the Peloponnesian War in 416 B.C., Athens obliterated the island of Melos.[81] Men were summarily executed while women and children were sold into slavery. Later the island was repopulated by Athenians.[82] During the Punic Wars in 146 B.C., the Romans burned the city of Carthage. Out of the total population of 200 thousand, 150 thousand were wiped out. Young and healthy Carthaginian male captives were brought to the arena as gladiators to entertain the Roman nobility. Their situation was not very different from that of Black "Sambos" during slavery or Black athletes today in the United States.

In Medieval Europe religious and dynastic wars wiped out untold millions. King Philip II of Spain patronized the Inquisition against what he considered heresies. Jews in Spain and Portugal faced either conversion or expulsion. Those suspected of heresy were burned at the stake. The Huguenots and Albigenses in France were sent to the burning chamber.

As the result of religious persecution in Europe and subsequent mass migration, Protestantism became the basis of social order in the Americas and South Africa. European genocidal activities continued throughout the Napoleonic wars and reached its zenith during the First and Second World Wars.[83] The latest European genocide has come to be known as "ethnic cleansing" in Bosnia.

ASIA

During 1100 B.C. the Assyrian army obliterated the Hittite Kingdom. Its population was exterminated and its cities were razed to the ground. During 1300 A.D., Genghis Khan, the greatest ruler of the Mongol Empire, pursued a policy of mass destruction. His armored cavalry and archers massacred men, women, and children. Palaces and public buildings were burned. The Mongol Empire stretched from present day Korea to Vienna (Austria). In Asia the Ottoman Empire pursued a genocidal policy against Armenians, Greeks, and other minorities. Its guiding principle was, "Those who are innocent today might be guilty tomorrow."[84]

During the Second World War the Japanese murdered Koreans while the Chinese and Filipinos were reduced to slavery. Young Korean women were made to serve the sexual demands of Japanese soldiers. Asian genocide reached its zenith during the Vietnam War. Other notable genocidal activities in Asia were recently recorded in Indonesia, Cambodia, Iraq, Iran, Afghanistan, India, Pakistan, Bangladesh, Sri Lanka, and East Timor. Palestinians have exceeded their share of genocide.

THE AMERICAS

Genocide was an unknown notion to America's original inhabitants before the arrival of Christopher Columbus.[85] The Aztec nation occasionally offered human sacrifices to their gods. The post-Colombian era, however, changed the human character of the Americas.

While governor of the island of Hispaniola (Haiti and the Dominican Republic), Christopher Columbus massacred 50 thousand Indians and sold the rest into slavery. In 1519 Hernando Cortes ordered the destruction of the Aztec capital of Tenochtitlán (Mexico City). Approximately 350 thousand inhabitants perished while Cortes' conquistadors took all the gold to Spain. Aztec Emperor Montezuma committed suicide. For his services to the Spanish Crown, Cortes received 23 thousand Indians. In 1553, Francisco Pizarro, an illiterate pig breeder, captured Incan King Atahualpa, made him pay a ransom in gold and silver, and then decapitated him. Indians were chained at the neck and marched to toil in the gold and silver mines of Peru. Those who resisted were immediately decapitated. The conquistadors sometimes entertained themselves by slicing Indian women's breasts or feeding Indian babies to their dogs. By 1700 A.D., 80 thousand million Indians had perished.[86]

Indians were given to conquistadors as payment for distributing land in Latin America to the Spanish noblemen. They were treated as less than animals. One commentator likened Indians to "sardines in the sea" and "beasts of burden." Juan Gines de Sepulveda, one of the most respected theologians of his time, theorized that Indians deserved their treatment because "their sins were offensive to God." Abbee de Paw compared Indians to "dogs that couldn't bark, cows that couldn't be eaten, and impotent camels." The cross and the sword marched together in search for gold and silver. The Spanish Crown received one-fifth of the proceeds and priests received five percent of production in tithes in exchange for the absolution of the conquistadors' sins against humanity.

As slave trade and slavery were expanded in the Caribbean Islands and Latin America, Blacks were treated even worse than their decimated Indian "comrades in slavery." Cunning Blacks were punished by having their ears cut off, being beaten, burned alive, burned in slow fires, beheaded, thrown from precipices, crushed between cane-milling cylinders, or broken on a wheel. Pregnant women were often kicked in their bellies. In one memorable sermon to African slaves, a priest said, "My poor little ones, as slaves you have so many burdens to bear, but your soul remains free to fly one day to the happy mansions of the chosen."[87]

With the Haitian revolution, French General Leclerc, a brother-in-law of Napoleon Bonaparte, devised a plan to exterminate all Haitian Blacks except children under twelve. But because of "voodoo politics" and to the disappointment of his wife, Pauline Bonaparte, General Leclerc died before carrying out his Haitian Black genocide plan. It is no wonder that today's Haitian-on-Haitian violence has its historical roots in French colonial legacy.[88]

In what was to eventually become the United States, Indians met a similar genocidal fate. In Virginia, one of the first English colonies, settlers burned Indian towns and cornfields, murdered men, women, and children, and sold the rest into slavery. In New England, epidemics set the pace and the settlers finished the job. It is reported that General Andrew Jackson, who later became a United States president, personally supervised the mutilation of eight hundred Creek Indians, whom he referred to as savage dogs. Genocide against the Indian population throughout North America became the cornerstone of United States politics.[89]

While Blacks were not physically targeted during slavery because of their economic value, they were nevertheless subject to cultural genocide.[90]

Slave labor, arbitrary dissolution of family structure, slave breeding, interstate slave trade, subtle legalism, Anglo-Saxonization, and Christianization—all were and still are forms of genocide. In the antebellum South, the selective murders of a portion of Blacks for the purpose of exploiting the rest was a common occurrence. During the Reconstruction period, Blacks were lynched at a rate of one hundred per year. One politician in Georgia justified the lynching as follows, "A Black needs to be lynched and flogged to keep him from blaspheming the Almighty by his conduct, his smell and his color."[91] Other genocidal activities against Blacks included police harassment, economic exploitation, political intimidation, and psychological warfare. The Jim Crow laws stripped ex-slaves of their right to vote by instituting literacy tests, a poll tax, and the grandfather clause. In 1896 the United States Supreme Court upheld the doctrine of "separate but equal."

AFRICA

The notion of genocide in pre-colonial Africa was relatively alien, though certain tribes might have practiced limited human sacrifices to satisfy their gods. Africa, however, is the continent which has suffered most from all forms of genocide.

In 1884 Chancellor Otto Bismark convened the Berlin Conference. It was here that the partition of Africa was sanctioned. Great Britain and France allotted themselves a lion's share. The vast Congo was given as a gift to Belgian King Leopold I. In reality, multinational capitalists, the led by the British, exploited the mineral-rich Congo. Belgians were mere workers. The rest of Africa was divided among smaller European powers (Italy, Portugal, and Spain). Germany and Russia were essentially interested in expansion within eastern Europe, while the United States' expansion lay in the Western hemisphere, except for the artificially dependent "slave state" of Liberia, with its capital named Monrovia (after United States President James Monroe). Although Egypt and Ethiopia remained nominally independent, they were reduced to the European powers "protectorate" status.

Nineteenth century Africa, like the Americas earlier, became a hunting ground for cheap labor, raw materials, and a piece of real estate. Africans were captured, chained, and transported to work in the diamond and gold mines of South Africa, copper mines of the Congo, Zambia, and Zimbabwe, cocoa plantations of Ghana, Firestone rubber plantations of Liberia, and coffee plantations of Egypt and Sudan. Whether it was in African mines or on Virginian plantations, African people were mistreated, malnourished, overworked, and neglected. German colonists in southwest Africa (Namibia) almost annihilated ethnic Herero.[92]

NEO-COLONIAL GENOCIDE

The 1960s marked the end of colonialism in Africa and the beginning of a vicious form of neo-colonialism in which a self-styled, Western-educated, pseudo-elite became the instrument through which a neo-colonizer exploited and enslaved the neo-colonized. By inciting one ethnic group against the other or one religious group against the other, modern Africa became the scene of a series of genocidal activities.

In the early 1960s Africa witnessed genocidal activities in the Congo. The Cold War shoulders a part of the blame. The second half of the 1960s saw genocidal activities in the Nigeria-Biafran War which began as an inter-ethnic power struggle between the Igbos and the Housas. During the first half of the 1970s, inter-ethnic genocidal activities took place in Burundi.[93] There was a man-made famine in Ethiopia in the latter half of the 1970s. Meanwhile, Angola, Uganda,

ınued their genocidal activities. In the 1980s Africa
:idal activities in Somalia and Liberia. The 1990s will
l as a time of genocide in Burundi and Rwanda.

.or of today's African rulers is not strikingly different from that of the seventeenth century African kings who sold their people into slavery for a bottle of rum. Today's African rulers sell their people into neo-colonial slavery for Cadillacs, presidential planes, or villas abroad. As Marcus Garvey once remarked, "Africans are their own enemies."

TABLE 1.
SELECTED CHRONOLOGY OF GENOCIDE IN EUROPE[94]

Country	*Date*	*Perpetrators*	*Victims*	*Est. No.*
Melos	146 B.C.	Athenian Army	Melians	Unknown
Carthage	146 B.C.	Roman Army	Carthaginians	150,000
Ottoman Empire	1915–22	Ottoman Army	Armenians	1,000,000
Soviet Union	1932–37	Soviet Army	Ukrainians	10,000,000
Germany	1939–45	Nazi Army	Jews	6,000,000
			Gypsies	50,000
			Others	4,000,000

TABLE 2.
SELECTED CHRONOLOGY OF GENOCIDE IN ASIA

Country	*Date*	*Perpetrators*	*Victims*	*Est. No.*
China	1211–34	Ghengis Khan	Chinese	Unknown
		Mongols	Muslims	
Iraq	1959–75	Iraqi Army	Kurds	Unknown
Indonesia	1965–67	Indonesian Army	Communists	600,000
Vietnam	1965–72	US Army	Viet-Cong	Unknown
			S. Vietnamese	
Bangladesh	1971	E. Pakistani Army	Bengalis	3,000,000
Cambodia	1975–79	Khmer Rouge	Old regime	2,000,000
Afghanistan	1978–79	Regular Army	Rebels	Unknown
Iran	1981–90	Regular Army	Kurds	
			Bahai	
			Mujahedeen	20,000
Sri-Lanka	1983–87	Regular Army	Tamil	10,000
East Timor	1975–?	Indonesian Army	Tomolese	100,000

TABLE 3.
SELECTED CHRONOLOGY OF
GENOCIDE IN THE AMERICAS

Country	*Date*	*Perpetrators*	*Victims*	*Est. No.*
Colonial	1492–	Spaniards	Indians	Unknown
America	1789	Portuguese		
		British		
		French		
United States	1789-1900	Regular army	Indians	Unknown
		Militia		
Paraguay	1962–72	Regular army	Ache Indians	9,000
Guatemala	1966–84	Regular army	Indians	60,000
			Leftists	
Chile	1963–76	Regular army	Leftists	30,000
Argentina	1976–80	Regular army	Leftists	30,000
El Salvador	1980–?	Regular army	Leftists	70,000

TABLE 4.
SELECTED CHRONOLOGY OF GENOCIDE IN AFRICA

Country	Date	Perpetrators	Victims	Est. No.
Namibia	1904	German Troops	Herero	65,000
Sudan	1952–94	Regular army	Black animists	Unknown
		Islamic North	Christians	
Angola	1961–?	Regular army	UNITA	Unknown
Rwanda	1959–94	Regular army	Abatutsi	Unknown
Congo/Leo	1964–65	Regular army	Lumumbists	Unknown
Nigeria	1966–70	Regular army	Igbos	3,000,000
Burundi	1972	Regular Army	Hutu Rebellion	Unknown
Uganda	1976–78	Regular army	Opposition	500,000
Mozambique	1975–94	Regular army	RENAMO	Unknown
Ethiopia	1984–85	Regular army	Opposition	Unknown
Somalia	1988–89	Regular army	Opposition	Unknown
Liberia	1990–94	Regular army	Rebels	Unknown

3

A Theoretical Framework of Genocide

The Torah is the source of the Jewish myth of being the chosen people. The Bible is the primary source of the Euro-American myth of racial superiority. The Koran is the primary source of Arab myth. Hinduism provides myth for the Hindus. Buddhism provides the Sacred Truth for the people of China, Japan, Burma, Thailand, Cambodia, Laos, Ceylon, and many other parts of Asia. Maybe it is time that Africans[95] develop their own written Sacred Truth.

5

BIBLICISM

JUDAISM

Judaism is believed to have begun six thousand years ago. It is known to be the origin of monotheism. In Hebrew cosmogenic myth, YHVH[96] created everything in six days. Judaic beliefs are enshrined in the Torah. The Torah was one of the first few documents written soon after the invention of writing in Sumaria 3000–1500 B.C. It was developed from Babylonian and Chaldean myths. Its unknown authors are simply referred to as J (Jehovah), E (Elohim), D (Deutoronomist), and P (Priestly), according to the period in which the documents were written. Some of the stories in the Torah are based on historical facts while others are works of fiction.

The Hebrew Yahweh is portrayed as the Holy Creator, the Sustainer, and the Redeemer—a perfect and powerful God. But Yahweh is also depicted as a god of hate whose vengeance and cruelty is limitless, and whose malice inflicts pain and grief; a deity that frightens people into obedience, causes storms, earthquakes, famine, and plagues. He gives either infinite rewards or infinite torments. He does evil or causes evil to be done. Yahweh's unlimited cruelty is consistent throughout the Old Testament.

Case 1. Yahweh vs. Adam and Eve

For stealing a forbidden apple, Adam and Eve and their descendents were condemned to forced labor in perpetuity.

> I will multiply your pain
> In the sweat of your face you shall eat bread
> You are dust and to dust you shall return. (Genesis 3:16-19)

To this day we are still serving the sentence.

Case 2. Yahweh vs. Cain

Yahweh caused Cain to murder his younger brother, Abel, and then condemned him to become a vagabond forever.

Case 3. Yahweh vs. Noah

For its prevailing sinful condition, the vengeful Yahweh annihilated the known world. He confided to Noah:

> I will destroy man whom I have created from the face of the earth;
> Men with beasts, creeping things and birds of the sky . . .
> (Genesis 6:6-7)

Then:

> . . . the fountains of the great deep broken up
> And windows of heavens were opened (Genesis 7:11)

The flood lasted forty days and nights, destroying every living thing. Afterwards, a remorseful Yahweh blessed Noah's sons:

> Be fruitful and multiply
> Swarm on earth and increase thereon (Genesis 8)

Case 4. Yahweh vs. Abraham

For the sake of creating crises, the capricious Yahweh caused Abraham[97] to lie twice about his wife and to his long-awaited son, Isaac. Yahweh also caused him to commit adultery with Hagar and then to expel her and her son Ishmael from his household. Yahweh ignored Abraham's intercession on behalf of Sodom and Gommorah and proceeded to firebomb the twin cities.

Case 5. Yahweh vs. Moses

In the process of delivering the Israelites from Egyptian slavery, Yahweh caused plagues and drowned the Egyptian army in the Red Sea. For worshipping the golden calf, Yahweh punished the Israelites with famine and made them wander aimlessly in the Sinai desert for forty years. The promised land of "milk and honey" became a nightmare. For instituting the worship of a brazen serpent, Yahweh caused Moses[98] to mysteriously disappear without ever reaching the promised land.

Case 6. Yahweh vs. King David

The unpredictable Yahweh caused King David[99] to commit adultery with Bathsheba, then punished him by dismantling his dynasty.

Case 7. Yahweh vs. Job

Yahweh, who delights himself in crises, permitted Satan to destroy Job's estate and afflict him with a form of leprosy. Job, who is portrayed in the Old Testament as a man of faith, began to wonder why the untrustworthy Yahweh gives life to whom he intends misery and bitterness:

> Naked I came from my mother's womb
> And naked shall I return;
> The Lord gave, and the Lord has taken away (Job 1:21)

Then he cursed the day he was born:

> That day let it be darkness (Job 1:21)

Case 8. Yahweh vs. The Prophets

The vengeful Yahweh continued to play an important role in Jewish history by administering rewards and punishments. Through the prophets Yahweh inspired fear and demanded submission:

> Fear and the pit are upon thee inhabitants of the earth
> (Isaiah 24:17)

> To me every knee shall bow
> Every tongue shall swear (Isaiah 45:23)

Case 9. Yahweh vs. Jesus

Yahweh, who delighted himself in sadistic and masochistic acts, delivered his "only begotten son" into the hands of a corrupt Jewish aristocracy in collusion with Roman imperialism. During his last agony, Jesus wondered why his father (Abba) had abandoned him:

> Eli, Eli, Lama Sabachthani

Translation:

> My God, my God, Why has thou forsaken me
> (Compare Matthew 27:46 and Psalms 22:1)

Judaism rejects Jesus' divine status and opposes the Christian concept of Original Sin.

JUDEO-CHRISTIANITY

Christianity is an offshoot of Judaism. It appropriated Judaic dogmas, legends, and certain rites with some variations. If there is anything Christians agree upon, it is the controversial two natures (homoousis) of Jesus Christ: Human (hupostatis) and Divine (prospon). The first nature is historical, thus descriptive. The second nature is metaphysical, thus speculative.

Historical Jesus
(Hebrew=Yshua; Greek=Iesous)

The historical Jesus was born to Joseph and Mary[100] in a barn in the small village of Nazareth of Galilee, seventy miles from Jerusalem. His father was a poor carpenter, his mother an ordinary housewife. The fact that they brought two turtle doves to the temple to sacrifice on his behalf indicates the state of their economic and social status.

Little is recorded of Jesus' education, but like his followers, he probably had little formal education. Annas, one of the members of the Jewish aristocratic Council characterized John and Peter as unlearned and ignorant. Some biblical scholars speculate that Jesus spent some time in the Himalayan (India) monasteries studying the scriptures under Brahman priests. Others speculate that he was a member of the Essenes Community in Galilee.

Like any young Jew of his generation, Jesus was married with children. According to Barbara Thiering, Jesus was married to Mary Magdalene and had a son, Merovée, who, according to legend, is believed to be the founder of the French Merovingian dynasty. Jesus later divorced Mary Magdalene and remarried Lydia.

At age thirty, stirred by John the Baptist's reform movement, Jesus traveled from Nazareth to be baptized in the Jordan River. He withdrew into the wilderness for prayer, meditation, and soul-searching. Although little is recorded on what motivated Jesus to begin a public ministry, the arrest and subsequent beheading of his cousin, John the Baptist, must have been an important factor in his decision.

Unlike John the Baptist, Jesus became an activist.[101] He selected an inner circle of twelve disciples[102] to represent the twelve tribes of Judah. Jesus became an itinerant preacher, traveling to the towns and villages along the Sea of Galilee. His listeners were the people he met haphazardly on the roadsides. He attracted the destitute and prostitutes, lepers and outcasts, helpless and homeless. He preached in an Aramaic dialect, using parables understood by ordinary people. He practiced exorcism, healed the sick, raised the lame, ordered away unclean spirits, and performed miracles. Each miracle increased his popularity.

Jesus' eschatological message of the Kingdom of God was not new. Isaiah had preached a similar message in a similar political predicament seven centuries before. Instinctively, Jesus identified himself with the oppressed. He was also aware of Jewish aristocratic indifference. He attacked the hypocrisy of pharisees for swallowing the widow's property, amassing wealth, and then saying long prayers. His message was understood by ordinary Jews.

His popularity worried the Sanhedrin (Jewish aristocratic community) and irritated Roman colonists. Fearing a pre-emptive Roman strike, the Sanhedrin plotted to arrest and try Jesus in religious court. "It is expedient for us, that one man should die . . . that the whole nation perish not," declared the Chief Priest.

In 30 A.D. Jesus was arrested and briefly tried. He was accused of having claimed to be the "Son of God with the power to forgive sins and bring about the Kingdom of God"—an accusation that constituted a blasphemy which was punishable by death. He was then, according to law, handed over to Pontius Pilate for formal sentencing. After a brief appearance, Jesus was sentenced to death by crucifixion, the Roman standard of capital punishment. Crucifixion continued to be a part of Roman law until its abolition by Emperor Constantine.

Jesus underwent a process of mental and physical cruelty. His hands were tied above his head. He was spit on and insulted. He was bayoneted. He endured the mandatory thirty-nine lashes with a custom-made whip known as a "cat of nine tails." Then, sadistic and masochistic Roman soldiers ordered him to carry a heavy cross with the mocking inscription: JNRI (Jesus the King of Jews).

Jesus, weakened by torture and pitifully staggering along, could barely carry the cross. Roman soldiers ordered an African bystander,

Simon of Cyrene, to help him. Jesus was crucified in Golgotha between two notorious thieves, Titus and Dumachus. Before Jesus' death, he experienced ordinary human psychological agony and blamed God for failing to intervene on his behalf. That was the end of Jesus and the beginning of Jesus Christ.

METAPHYSICAL JESUS

Since Jesus left no writing of his own, any attempt to reconstruct his biography depends on the accounts of the four canonical Gospels attributed to Matthew, Mark, Luke, and John. The first three Gospels are often referred to as synoptic Gospels because of their similarities. Their authors are unknown. The names attributed to them might be fraudulent. Their stories are probably pious legends.

The myth of metaphysical Jesus[103] begins with Mary Magdalene. Refusing to believe that her lover's death was definite, she went to the tomb early one morning. In a state of hallucination, Mary Magdalene mistook a farmer to be the risen Christ. She cried out, "Rabboni" (Teacher), and ran to embrace him. The beleaguered farmer told her not to touch him. Disappointed, Mary Magdalene left in a hurry and spread the news of Jesus' resurrection. Peter and James confirmed it. Jesus' followers accepted it. This story is carefully recorded in the Gospels, proselytized through the efforts of the Apostles, and reaffirmed by Apostle Paul's[104] tireless missionary work. Today, the story of Jesus is accepted by millions of human souls throughout the world.

The Gospel of Mark

The author of the Gospel of Mark is not interested in Jesus' birth and childhood. He begins with Jesus' baptism and is eager to prove that Jesus Christ was indeed the Son of God and supports his thesis by quoting Isaiah 40:3 instead of Malachi 3:1:

> I will send my messenger and
> He shall prepare the way before me

Moreover, he fictionalizes the events surrounding Jesus' baptism:

> After the Baptism, the heavens split open;
> The Holy Spirit descended on Jesus like a dove;
> and he heard a voice from heaven saying
> thou art my beloved Son; with thee I am well pleased
> (Mark 1:11)

Mark records the myth of Jesus' transfiguration on the mountain while accompanied by Peter, James, and John:

> . . . his face shone like the sun, his clothes became white as the light
> . . . Moses and Elijah talking to him and heard a voice from heaven
> . . . this is my beloved son in whom I am well-pleased (Mark 9:2-32)

The author also portrays Jesus as the Son of Man who will return in glory:

> I am, and you will see the son of man
> seated at the right hand of power and with the clouds of heaven
> (Mark 14:61-64)

The Gospel of Matthew

The author of the Gospel of Matthew edits and revises the text of Mark. He is interested in the theory of virginal conception and messianic royalty of Jesus Christ through the line of King David:

> . . . Judah begat Phares (Perez)
> of Thamar (Tamar)
> (Compare Matthew 1:3, Genesis 38:15, and I Chronicles 2:4)
>
> . . . Boaz begat Obed
> . . . of Ruth . . . (Matthew 1:5)
>
> David the King begat Solomon[105]
> . . . of Bathsheba . . . (Compare 2 Samuel 11 and Matthew 1:6)

And he supports his thesis by quoting Isaiah 1:11:

> A shoot shall come out from the stump of Jesse,
> and a branch shall grow out of his roots

But the four women mentioned in Jesus' genealogy were more immoral than royal.

The Gospel of Luke

The author of the Gospel of Luke edits and elaborates on the Gospels of Matthew and Mark. He supports his thesis on virginal conception and messianic royalty by quoting Isaiah and Micah:

> . . . Behold, a virgin shall conceive, and bear a son,
> And shall call his name Emanuel . . . (Isaiah 7:14-25)

... his name shall be Wonderful
Counselor, Might God, Everlasting father,
Prince of Peace (Isaiah 11:1)

... Out of thee shall he come forth into me
that is to be ruler of Israel ... (Micah 5:3)

Both authors of the Gospels of Matthew and Luke are interested in the transcendental importance of Jesus Christ by retraction. But they contradict themselves by de-emphasizing Jesus' biological father.

The Gospel of John

The author of the Gospel of John has little interest in Jesus' virginal conception or messianic royalty. For him, Jesus is the Word incarnate, the Lamb of God, the only begotten Son of God. Jesus' crucifixion and resurrection are manifestations of God's love. Jesus Christ is defined as a divine radiance and the glory of God:

In the beginning was the Word
And the Word was with God
And the Word was God (John 1:1)

Jesus is Christ, the son of God
And through his faith you may possess life by his name
(John 20:30)

His name is called the word of God (Revelation 19:13)

The Word was made flesh ...
Only begotten by the Father ... (John 1:14)

Behold the lamb of God
Which takes away the sin of the world
(Compare John 1:29 and Isaiah 52:7)

I am the Good Shepherd
(Compare John 10:11 and Ezekiel 34:11-12)

I and my Father are one (John 10:30)

The crucified Jesus is metaphorically compared to Moses' crucified brazen serpent and a lamb before the slaughter:

> As Moses lifted up the serpent in the wildness,
> even so must the Son of Man be lifted up. (John 3:15)

> He was despised and rejected;
> . . . a man of suffering.
> He was wounded for our transgressions
> (Compare John 12:38 and 53:1-4)

For the author of the Gospel of John, Jesus Christ was not born by sexual impulse or through human paternity.

Apostle Paul

Apostle Paul's writings are in the form of letters. About one-fourth of the New Testament was written by him and he is the center of interest in the Acts of Apostles. Apostle Paul claimed to have encountered metaphysical Jesus Christ in a vision and ecstatic trances:

> I was in trance and . . . saw Him (Acts 22:17).

He claims that his ideas came through revelation:

> I neither received it from man nor was I taught it,
> but it came through the revelation of Jesus Christ.
> (Galatians 1:11-12)

As a theorist, Apostle Paul elaborated on the concept of grace, faith, salvation, Original Sin, and the separation of soul and body. He raised the cosmic issues on the struggle between good and evil, flesh and spirit, faith and work, and grace and merit. Although he refers to Jesus Christ's redemptive death and resurrection, he remains silent on his divinity. For Paul, Jesus' resurrection was a transformation from physical to spiritual existence.

ORTHODOX AND HETERODOX THEORY

By the end of the first century, Jerusalem, the original Christian headquarters, had been sacked. A decentralized urban system of Bishoprics had been established and the Apostles' writings were among the best known in the Christian community. Christian theorists continued to debate, edit, and formulate ideas which gradually shaped European society and culture.

Orthodox theorists affirmed the writings in the Gospels and Apostle Paul's Epistles stressed the concept of One God, and the doctrine of Trinity. Irenaeus, one of the earliest theorists, wrote that Jesus was born, suffered, died, and rose again. He believed that Jesus was the true Adam and that those who shared Adam's humanity also shared his act of sinning as well as his penalty; and those who believed in Christ shared with him the reward of a redeemed humanity. He taught that while the Father is unbegotten, the Son is the only begotten.

At the Council of Nicaea in 325 A.D., Jesus Christ was defined as having the same substance as the Father—the true God—begotten and not created. The Nicene Creed reads as follows:

> We believe in One God,
> The father All Governing (Pantokrata)
> Creator (Poieten) of All things, visible and invisible
> and in One Lord Jesus Christ, the Son of God
> Begotten of the Father as only begotten
> From the essence (reality) of the Father (ek tes ousias tou patros)
> God from God, Light from Light
> True God from True God
> Begotten not created (Poiethenta)
> Of the essence (reality) as the Father (homoousion to patri)
> Through whom all things came into being
> Both in heaven and on earth;
> Who for us men and for our salvation
> Came down and was incarnate
> Being human (enantropesanta)
> He suffered and the third day he rose,
> And ascended into and heavens
> And he will come to judge both
> The living and the dead
> And we believe in the Holy Spirit

Gradually the Nicene Creed became a measurement of Christianity. St. Ambrose wrote, "Moses' words were God's words," and St. Thomas Aquinas believed, "Nothing was made by God after the six days of creation." Galileo was forced to denounce his theory which was believed to contradict the teaching of Christianity. As late as

1900, Pope Pius IX declared, "Darwinism contradicts the revealed revelations of creation to the Creator," and Bishop Samuel Wilberforce declared, "Darwinism was repugnant to history and to reason itself."

The Nicene Creed and the condemnations of Arianism did not discourage the spread of Gnostic ideas. Gnostic theorists continued to challenge the spiritual authority of orthodox Christianity. The controversy issues centered on the divinity and resurrection of Jesus Christ, the divinity of the Holy Spirit, and the status of the Virgin Mary (Theotokos).

Heterodox theorists were often denounced as the followers of Simon Magus who had earlier claimed to be the power of God (dynamis) and that Helen, his mistress, was a reincarnation of the Spirit of God (Ennoi). He considered Jesus Christ's death and resurrection to be a mere appearance and rejected the Old Testament as fraudulent and malicious. Arius thought that Jesus Christ was created and not eternally begotten. Other heterodox theorists thought of Jesus Christ as an ordinary man (psilos, antropos) with ordinary human desires and instincts (consupiscentia). Nestorians emphasized Jesus Christ's humanity and rejected the concept that the Virgin Mary was the Mother of God (Theotokos). Monophysites rejected the dual nature in Christ.

Heterodox theorists believed in a God who is unknown, unknowable, and inaccessible, and from whom emanates subordinate gods (aeons). These emanations, Gnostics thought, constituted pleroma. They rejected the theory of virginal conception and the concept of Original Sin. Jesus' crucifixion, resurrection, and ascension was considered an art of fiction. For the heterodox theorist, salvation could come only from knowledge (gnosis).

CHRISTIAN PERSECUTION

Until the unexpected conversion of Emperor Constantine in 313 A.D., Christianity was considered *religio illicita*. Christians constituted a hated class.[106] Christians were accused of infanticide, cannibalism, incest, black magic, atheism, perverse, and subversive. Christians were even blamed for natural disasters. Their churches were destroyed, their books confiscated or burned, and their leaders were made martyrs, imprisoned, or exiled. During the summer of 64 A.D. when a fire destroyed Rome, Christians were named as the scapegoat.

But Christianity also found true believers. Some defended their faith to their death. Apostle Stephen, while being stoned to death, is reported to have said:

> Behold, I see the heavens open
> And the Son of Man standing on
> the right hand of God. (Acts 7:56)

He asked Christ to receive his spirit and forgive his tormentors. Ignatius, the Bishop of Antioch, was even dramatic. He visualized himself of becoming a Eucharist:

> I wish to taste the bread of God
> which is the flesh of Jesus Christ;
> and drink the blood which is an immortal drink . . .
> Let me be fodder for wild beasts . . .
> I am God's wheat and
> I am being ground by teeth of wild beasts
> to make a pure loaf for Christ . . .
> If I suffer, I shall be emancipated by Jesus Christ
> and united to him . . .
> What I want is God's bread,
> which is the flesh of Christ . . .
> and drink I want his blood . . . .
> An immortal love feast
> (Romans 1, 2, 4, 5, 6, 7, 8)

Polycarp, the Bishop of Smyrna, while being tied to a post in the pyre, thought of himself as "sharing the cup of Christ" with other martyrs. Perhaps the most dramatic affirmation of faith was the case of two young women Perpetua and Felicitas of Carthage in Africa. They were accused of being Christians and, hence, sentenced to die. As they were led into the amphitheater for execution, Perpetua behaved as if she was the bride of Christ and Felicitas entertained the idea of fighting the beasts and that her martyrdom would be transformed into her second baptism.

But legalization alone did not end intra-Christian persecution. In the Middle Ages the Catholic Church itself became persecutor and prosecutor (excommunicamus et damnamus). The penalty for a suspected heretic was death by burning (animadversio). The horror stories of Christian crusades and the Inquisition are documented in thousands of volumes. Perhaps the most dramatic cases were the

1431 burning of Joan of Arc at the stake as a heretic, and the Saint Bartholomew massacre in which Protestant Huguenots in Paris were mutilated and Pope Gregory XIII celebrated with a Te Deum.

JUDEO-CHRISTIANITY VS. AFRICANITY

Racial prejudice did not spring from a vacuum. It is anchored in thousands of years of acculturation. Judaic writings tell us that blackness is a symbol of something hateful. Blacks are depicted as the seed of the cursed Cain or the descendants of the cursed Ham:

> Canaan's children shall be born ugly and Black,
> their hair kinky, their lips swell.
> They will be thieves and fornicators.
> They will be banded together in hatred of their masters
> and never tell the truth.

In Hebrew mythology, blackness symbolizes bitterness (Job 2:5; Joel 2:6; Isaiah 50:3, Hebrew 12:18), anything hateful (Job 3:4-9), a course of sin (Proverbs 2:13, Ephesians 5:17), affliction (Job 23:13, Psalms 112:41, Ecclesiastes 5:17), destruction, death, and under- world (Psalms 1143:3, Isaiah 5:30, Job 13:13), and curse and punish- ment (Deuteronomy 28:29, Psalms 35:6, Joel 2:2, Amos 5:18, I Kings 8:12 Psalms 104:20). In contrast to blackness, whiteness represents godliness, light, and purity (Psalm 104:2, 4:6, Revelation 22:5, Isaiah 42:10, I John 1:5-7, John 8:12). In the Song of Solomon, an erotic poem, a Black princess is depicted defending her blackness before light-skinned interlocutors:

> Nigra sum sed fumosa
> Tusca sum et fomosa
> Negra sum et speciosa

When this Latin text is translated into English, some transla- tors prefer the conjunction *and* while others prefer the conjunc- tion *but*. The conjunction *and* makes the text complimentary while the conjunction *but* makes the text denigrating to black- ness. Compare the following translations:

> I am black and beautiful
> But do not look at me
> Because I am blackened
> I am Black like the tents of Kedar

Versus:

> I am black but comely
> As the tents of Kedar
> As the curtains of Solomon
> Look not upon me
> Because I am Black.

Apostle Paul insisted on the inconsequence of race, culture, and class:

> Circumcised and uncircumcised,
> There cannot be Greek or Jew
> Barbarian and Synthia
> Slave and Free man
> But Christ is all, and in all (Galatians 3:28)

Christianity perpetuated negative images of blackness through the New Testament. The Christian God was portrayed as an elderly White man seated on a white throne, surrounded by blonde-haired, blue-eyed angels. The Virgin Mary is painted as a White mother holding a White baby Jesus. Satan is depicted as the prince of darkness surrounded by Black imps.

African slave trade and slavery amplified Black-White dichotomy. The Bible was interpreted to justify slavery and to make an African a perfect slave. Color consciousness became a psychological obsession and social parameter. In 1680 the Anglican Church accepted the theory that slavery was compatible with Christianity. Christian theorists argued that Christianity and African slavery were compatible and that slavery had been ordained by God. A favorite sermon of slave-owning Whites was an exhortation to African slaves to be obedient and have faith in their masters. The American Southern Baptist Convention was founded in defense of slavery. It was not until 1995 that the Convention announced publicly its sin of "condoning and perpetuating systematic racism." As recently as 1996, Barnetts Creek Baptist Church in Thomasville, Georgia, USA, refused to bury an infant of a mixed-race couple.

Color imagery was highlighted further in the interpretation of Scriptures and writings of Hymns. Hymns, carefully crafted to brainwash unsuspecting masses, reinforced color dichotomy.

In Baptist Hymnal #89 "Jesus Paid It All," phrases such as, "I will wash my garments white in Calvary's lamb; He washed it white as snow," are often stressed. In "Are You Washed in the Blood," phrases such as, "Are your robes white; Are your garments spotless, Are they white as snow?" are repeatedly emphasized. In Hymn #145 "Just As I Am," the phrase, "To rid my soul of one dark blot" is stressed. In Hymn #151, "He Lifted Me," the phrase, "From the shades of night to plains of light," night implies blackness or darkness and light implies whiteness. In Hymn #169, "Though your sins be as scarlet, they shall be as white as snow . . . though they be red like crimson, they will be as white as wool," scarlet, white as snow, red like crimson, white as wool are stressed. In Hymn #170, "Are You Washed in the Blood," verse after verse depicts the dichotomy of blackness and whiteness. Blackness has been metaphorically linked to sin and whiteness to salvation.

Jesus is portrayed to have come into this world to make Blacks "radiantly bright" and only through the shining grace of Christ, the outer blackness can be transformed into "inner whiteness." The Christian concept of "cleansing" implies removal of blackness, as sin is synonymous with blackness. Calvinism, however, condemned blackness (negritude) as predestined to eternal damnation. Meanwhile, Sir John Newton, the author of the most popular Christian Hymn "Amazing Grace," transformed his sweet melodies into amazing riches by trading African flesh. One of his slave ships was even baptized Jesus.

Amazing Grace, How Sweet the sound
That Saved a wretch like me!
I was once lost, but now I am found
Was Blind, but now I see.

CHRISTIANITY IN AFRICA

In Africa the Catholic tradition was executed to the letter. Africans were forced to accept baptism as their sole salvation. Sunday was declared a day of rest and worship. Those found working on Sundays were severely punished and their tools confiscated. The Catholic Church introduced the worship of images of Jesus Christ, the Virgin Mary, and the Patron Saints. Medals and rosaries were sold over the counter. Converts were forbidden to read or possess the Bible. The Mass was conducted in Latin, even in remote villages.

Missionaries sought to impose their own beliefs, values, and attitudes by attacking African spirituality. Recruited from the lowest strata in their respective societies and often uneducated, they entertained the idea of being superior to even powerful African kings. Africans were collectively referred to as "pagans" and their religion was seen as a satanic cult. African converts were depicted as "little boys." French missionaries had the habit of referring to the native priests with the French familiar pronouns, *tu* and *toi*, instead of the formal *vous*, reserved for respectable personalities.

A typical Christian mission in rural Africa consisted of an imposing church surrounded by a primary school and hospital or dispensary. Each was complimentary to one another—the church to colonize the African soul; the school to colonize the African mind; and the hospital to cure the African body for the benefit of colonial labor.

Convinced that Africans were incapable of understanding Christian theological concepts, European missionaries taught their converts to memorize the Ten Commandments:

Thou shalt have no other gods before me

Thou shalt not make unto thee my graven image

Thou shalt not take the name of the Lord thy God in vain

Remember the Sabbath day, to keep it holy

Honor they father and thy mother

Thou shalt not kill

Thou shalt not commit adultery

Thou shalt not steal

Thou shalt not bear false witness against thy neighbor

Thou shalt not covet thy neighbor's house

The Lord's Prayer and the art of making the sign of the cross became daily rituals before meals and bedtime.

Opposition to Catholicism was a punishable offense. African traditional religious leaders, such as *abapfumu* in Burundi, were hunted and imprisoned. Their religious objects were confiscated and publicly burned. The Catholic Church introduced its own religious rituals such as holy water, incenses, novenas, candles, and confession boxes. The Eucharist became the most popular sacrament.

Promising men and women were lured into monasteries and convents in a country where celibacy was considered a disgrace. Intermarriage between Catholic and non-Catholic persons was forbidden. Offenders of the Catholic code of behavior were sentenced to hell. Minor offenses were to carry, at the discretion of a priest, a suspended sentence in purgatory. The righteous, those who paid their regular tithes, were promised eternal life. Confessions were a private matter between the sinner and the confessor—the latter holding a key to the former's fate. In the process, sexual assault and homosexuality were recorded.

Dressed up in their Sunday best, converts converged at various mission stations for services. Some were attracted by hummed hymns which were no more than harmonized noise. Others went to socialize and listen to the latest rumors.

Protestant missions had more money. Protestant ethics were stricter than Catholic ethics. Rules governing smoking, drinking, and sexuality were reinforced. Protestants encouraged reading the Bible. Unlike the rigid Catholic hierarchy and the infallibility of the Pope, Protestantism was less structured and encouraged personal relationships with God. In philosophy and in practice, however, Protestantism in Africa reflected a "southern slave plantation mentality."

What is in a Name?

A name is not a mere label or tag—it has psychological impact on its bearer. In certain instances a name may shape an individual's character. Missionaries imposed European names on the unsuspecting as baptismal badges. In regions dominated by Saxons, English names such as Edward, Wilson, and Nelson were more popular. In regions dominated by Irish Catholics, Patrick was popular. In regions dominated by Italian missionaries, Pasqual was popular. Other baptismal names were chosen from among the Apostles, Saints, Bishops, and Popes.

BASIC CHRISTIAN BELIEFS

Christianity began as a Jewish sect. Its ideology is rooted in Hebrew mythology and enshrined in the Old and New Testaments. Some stories are based on facts, others are fiction or folklore parables. Basic Christian beliefs include the myths of Original Sin, incarnation, virgin birth, atonement and the Second Coming

According to Orthodox Christian views, we are all sinners and can be saved only if we believe in Jesus Christ (Romans 2:23, 5:12; John 14:6). Did Jesus make the claim that he was the only way to God? Such conditional salvation led to forced conversion and persecution. Christianity today is divided into:

1. Roman Catholicism. Roman Catholicism accepts the Bible as God's inspired revelation and the Catholic tradition as authoritative. Furthermore, Catholicism emphasizes papal ineffability and veneration of images.

2. Eastern Orthodox. Eastern Orthodox Christians accept the Bible as God's inspired revelation and its tradition as authoritative.

3. Protestantism. Protestantism accepts the Bible alone as the final authority in matters of faith and practices. Protestantism also stresses the liberty of conscience (libre examen) and the victory of private judgment. Protestantism is divided into many denominations.

All branches of Christianity believe in the doctrine of the Trinity (God, Son, and the Holy Spirit) and consider Jesus Christ to be both divine and human. Like any organized religion, Christianity is accepted as a matter of faith. One of the creeds which serves as an affirmation in both Methodist and Presbyterian churches reads:

I believe in God the Father Almighty
Maker of heaven and earth
I believe in Jesus Christ, his only Son, our Lord
Who was conceived by the Power of the Holy Spirit
Born of the Virgin Mary
Suffered under Pontius Pilate. Crucified, dead and buried
He descended into hell;
He rose again from the dead;
He ascended into heaven,
And sitteth on the right hand of God
He shall come to judge the quick and the dead
I believe in the Holy Ghost, the Holy Catholic Church,
. . . the communion of saints, the forgiveness of sins,
. . . the resurrection of the body and life everlasting. Amen.

Until the publication of Charles Darwin's[107] *The Origin of Species* in 1859, Christians believed that the universe was created by God in six days. St. Augustine, the Bishop of Hippo (North Africa) theorized, "Nothing is to be accepted save the authority of the Scriptures." St. Ambrose believed Moses' words were God's words. Thomas Aquinas thought, "Nothing was made by God after the six days of creation, absolutely nothing new."

In 1615 Galileo was brought before the Inquisition and forced to denounce his theory stating that the sun and not the earth was the center of the solar system. Similarly, Darwin's theory of natural selection was condemned by Pope Pius IX as a "contraction to the revealed relation of creation to Creator." Bishop Samuel Wiberforce also rejected Darwinism as repugnant to history and reason itself. He humorously wondered whether the human apelike ancestry originated with the grandfather or the grandmother.

As late as in the 1960s, the Bishop of the Ethiopian Orthodox Church (Abuna) doubted whether or not a man could walk on the moon. United States astronauts had just completed its mission. Today, Christianity is the dominant religion in Europe and the Americas, and has made substantial inroads in Africa and Asia. Christian churches dot rural landscapes and urban centers. Brooklyn, New York, USA, with an average of ten churches on every block, may claim to be the capital of Christianity. The southern part of the United States has been baptized as the "Bible belt."

JUDAIC ISLAM

Islam, like Christianity, sprang from Judaism during a period in which both Judaism and Christianity were in decline. Before the advent of Islam, Arab tribes worshipped idols and images, including the black stone of Kaaba in Mecca.

According to Islamic legend, Allah revealed himself to Muhammad through Angel Gabriel. As the Prophet Muhammad was illiterate, his supposed revelations were compiled in the Book of Qu'ran by his followers. The main themes found in the Qu'ran, such as the concepts of hell and heaven, are similar to those found in the Torah or Bible with minor interpretations.

Basic Islamic Beliefs

Islam opposed Judaism for worshipping golden calves and idols and opposed Christianity for worshipping Jesus Christ as God incarnate. Islam is divided into Sunnis, Shiah, and Suffis.

A good Muslim is expected to observe the five pillars of Islam. Muhammad's revelations and writings are compiled in the Book of Koran (recitation) which are believed to be the Word of Allah. The Koran teachings include:

1. Shadadah (Recitation)

2. Salah (Daily Prayer)

3. Zakat (Giving of Alms)

4. Fasting during the Month of Ramadan

5. Hajj (Pilgrimage to Mecca)

6

EUROCENTRISM

CLASSIC

During the Greek and Roman periods, little stigma was attached to skin color.[108] Differences in color were attributed to climate and geography. Greek art portrays Ethiopian gods with a black faces, flat noses, thick lips, and woolly hair. Thracians (Nordic) gods are portrayed with blue eyes and red hair. Anyone of the Greco-Roman culture was considered "barbarian." Herodotus, a Greek historian, described Ethiopians as people of woolly hair, as if they were Greek sheep. Solinis, a third century writer, described Ethiopians as filthy and compared them to dragons.

In Medieval Europe, blackness was linked to evil. During trans-Atlantic slave trade and thereafter, colorphobia became a determining factor in race relations. European colonists, missionaries, and travelers convinced themselves and others that racial groupings might have been created separately. Slave traders examined African captives as if they were animals. Africans were compared to apes in anatomy, gait, expression, and behavior. Blackness was linked to animal-like behavior, primitiveness, savagery, and brutishness.

In Shakespeare's *Othello*, blackness is linked to bestial sexuality. Today, blackness still carries negative connotations.[109] Blackness symbolizes mourning and grief. Black suits and dresses are worn at funerals. In contrast to blackness, whiteness symbolizes purity and beauty. White outfits are worn at baptisms and weddings.

MODERN

Monogenesis versus polygenesis theories on the origin of humankind abound. Eurocentrists strove to justify the natural inferiority of

Africans and the necessity to enslave them. In 1578 George Best theorized that blackness was caused by natural infection. In 1655 Isaac de la Peyrere rejected the biblical assumption of the single origin of mankind and suggested the possibility of multiple origins. He wrote that there may have been a pre-Adamite race from which Cain found a wife. Oliver Smith wrote that the original human species may have been White, and that blackness was a form of degeneration. James Cowles Prichard wrote that whiteness was a form of degeneration caused by climatic conditions. Others thought that the sun had scorched Africans, drawn their bile, and blackened their blood. But all failed to demonstrate how climate affected skin pigmentation.

Writing in *Journal des Scavans*, Leon Poliakov compared the hair of Africans to the Spaniels' (dog), and the eyes of Asians to pigs. Montesquieu linked blackness to moral and mental inferiority. Baron Cuvier, expressing commonly accepted European views, portrayed Black physical characteristics as "evidently approximate to monkey tribe." In his *Essaie sur l'inegalite des races humaines*, Joseph Arthur de Gobineau thought that physical characteristics such as color of skin, type of hair, and shape of skull were correlated with intelligence. Then he concluded Black intellectual faculties to be mediocre or non-existent.

In Carl Linneaus' 1730 theory, the "Great-Chain of Being," Black men were named as the missing link in the evolutionary process:

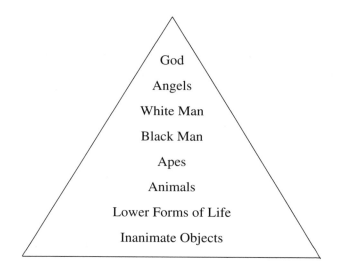

God
Angels
White Man
Black Man
Apes
Animals
Lower Forms of Life
Inanimate Objects

In 1748 Montesquieu wrote, "It is impossible to suppose that Blacks are men." David Hume wrote, "Negroes had neither arts nor sciences." In 1784 Crozat wrote in *Geographie Universelle*, "Negroes were well-built, but lazy, deceiving, drunken, greedy and dirty." In his 1786 *Notes on Virginia*, United States President Thomas Jefferson[110] wrote, "Negroes (Blacks) are inferior to the whites in the endowments in both body and mind," and that the Negro was "ugly with strong disagreeable odor and dull imagination." Voltaire, one of the eminent French philosophers, wrote that a Black person was "incapable of understanding philosophy or association of ideas."

Monogenesis and polygenesis theories continued to dominate nineteenth and early twentieth-century European thought. Francis Galton thought that intelligence, like height or the shape of noses or ears, was hereditary. His "Gaussian bell curve" charted foot length and head width. He concluded that measurements fell symmetrically on either side of the mean with a standard deviation. Galton believed that reaction time was associated with intelligence but could not prove his theory. In *Heredity and Genius* (1869), Galton wrote that the Negro intellect was "two grades below that of whites." In 1882 Francisque Sarcey described Blacks in *Les Races sauvages* as "bipeds, monkeylike, voracious descendants from gorillas who are devoid of moral sense and reason."

Darwin and Huxley believed that humans might have originated from a common apelike ancestor. But Richard Owen, whose anatomical collection included dogs, cats, mice, deer, and the head of an African person, opposed Darwin's evolutionary theory and advocated the theory of a polygenic origin of humankind. His hypothesis was based on the absence of the hippocampus minor in apes. Haeckel reasoned that Blacks were mentally nearer to apes and dogs. He portrayed a Black person as a speechless ape-man (Pithecanthropus alalus). Coon thought that Negroids (Congoids) were late in achieving brain size, thus backward and intellectually inferior. Eve theorists thought that modern humans originated in Africa and racial distinctions had little importance. Other racial theorists, such as Wolpoff and Thorne, believed in the multi-regionalism theory—that humans might have been developed simultaneously in various parts of the world.

In modern studies, reaction time is correlated with Intelligence Quotient (IQ) tests.[111] Various psychometricians believe that White reaction time is faster than Black reaction time. In 1901 Woodrow Wilson wrote, "Blacks were host of dusky children, insolent, sick of work and covetous of pleasure." In 1905 Dixon described a Black man as a "half child and half animal." Other pseudo-theorists stereotyped Blacks as criminals and mentally defective.

As recently as 1991, Jacques Chirac, then Mayor of Paris (now President of France) called North Africans an "overdose of welfare beams whose odors were an aggression against the French people." His predecessor, Giscard d'Estaing proposed *jus sanguinis*. These opinions were not opinions of ordinary people. They were opinions of people who engineered social policies.

Negrophobia phenomenon is not limited to Whites only. The pattern is widespread. Chinese students at Nanjing Hehai University attacked African students shouting, "Kill the black devils." In 1986 Japan's Prime Minister Yasuhiro Nakasone referred to Blacks as a "species of lower intelligence." Korean merchants in the Black ghettos of the United States treat their Black customers with contempt.

Social Darwinism

By the end of the nineteenth century Darwinism dominated European intellectual thinking. Although Darwinism and Social Darwinism are related, they differ in many respects.

Darwinism

Charles Darwin's theory of natural selection was based on the scientific premises that:

1. All living things increase their numbers at a prolific rate.

2. The size of a given organism remains constant.

3. Not all organisms produced in a given generation can survive, hence, the inescapable struggle for existence.

He concluded that the fittest organisms survive and pass their characteristics on to their offspring. For Darwin, species were mutable.

Social Darwinism

Social Darwinism recycled Darwin's theory of biology into social theory and applied it to human behavior. Herbert Spencer, an advocate of Social Darwinism, believed in a mysterious force upon which natural selection acts mechanically. He theorized that a society evolves like an organism and opposes government interference in the natural process. He also believed that the poor deserved to starve. William Graham Sumner, a Yale Sociology Professor, thought that natural selection must be left to take its course and poverty is the natural result of innate inferiority. He claimed, "Millionaires were the product of natural selection." John D. Rockefeller justified his business success as an example of "the survival of the fittest," the working of the law of nature, and the law of God. Pearson equated a race with a nation and wrote that the fittest nation would survive.

Social Darwinism rejected the Lamarchian view that individuals could improve themselves through education, health care, and better diet. To a Social Darwinian, individual fate is predetermined by the genes one inherits from ancestors.

Other racial theorists thought that differences in human intelligence, morality, esthetics, drive, and bravery were hereditary. They argued that the blonde, blue-eyed Anglo-Saxon (Teutonic) race was destined by natural selection to rule lower races. This prophecy persists today. The whiter one's skin, the fitter he or she was thought to be.[112] Africans found themselves at the bottom of the scale:

Anglo-Saxons
Latins
Slavs
Other Europeans
Asians
Africans

EUGENICISM

What began as a scientific theory of evolution was later transformed into the practice of genocide. Eugenicists believed that inferior races should not be permitted to prosper or reproduce. Various European countries enacted laws regulating sexual relations. Micengenation and sterilization laws were enforced. In the case of Buck vs. Bell, the United States Supreme Court upheld a sterilization law in Virginia to "prevent a generation of imbeciles." By the early twentieth century, behavioral psychologists adapted Social Darwinism to measure differences in intelligence among diverse racial groups. In 1934 Dr. Rene Martiel, a Lecturer at the University of Paris Faculty of Medicine, classified races according to genotypes by using a bio-chemical index of blood (groups A, B, AB, and O) and the formula:

$$\text{Intelligence} = \frac{fA+fAB}{fB+fAB}$$

Scores ran as follows: Alsatians 4.0; French 3.2; Germans 3.1; Dutch 3.0; Jews 1.6; Russians 1.4; Poles 1.2; and American Negro 0.9. Then Martiel concluded that Group A had character-istics of upright morality and courage, while group B was the very essence of baseness and evil. He recommended the elimination of every group below the 2.0 average. Otto Recke believed type A to be common among Northern Europeans; type B among Asians and Africans; and type O among American Indians. He proposed not to mingle A, B, and O blood types. Lewis Terman thought high intelligence was related to morality and success while low intelligence was correlated with criminality. In 1969 Arthur Jensen, a psychometrician, compared intelligence between Blacks and Whites by using the following formula:

$$IQ = \frac{\text{Mental Age} \times 100}{\text{Real Age}}$$

He concluded that differences in scores have genetic origin. In his 1992 study Jensen explored neurologic processing speed and claimed that smarter people process faster. In a 1991 review of literature on the African Black IQ, Richard Lynn estimated that the median African IQ was 75 points, 10 points below that of Black Americans. Colored IQ in South Africa was ranked with the Black American. According to Spearman's hypothesis, Whites excelled in spacial-perceptual ability while Blacks were better in retention and retrieval processes. In the 1994 review of IQ literature, Hernstein and Murray seem to agree that IQ is racially inherited. White psychometricians, however, fail to consider socio-economic factors. What they consider common knowledge is not. Comparing the IQs of African and Anglo-Saxon children is an exercise in absurdity, as is comparing the IQs of a Black child living in a Harlem ghetto to a Bushman child living in the Kalahari Desert.

Notes

1.   Genocide comes from the Greek word *genos,* which means race or tribe, and the Latin word *cide,* which means to kill. Genocide is defined as *the destruction of an ethnic group or nation.*

2.   Mwami Mutara Rudahirwa was crowned in 1953. He abolished the institution of *ubuhake* and the traditional practice of physical punishment. He is remembered as an imposing and progressive monarch. He encouraged education and established Fonds Mutara (scholarships for bright Rwandese students). He died in Bujumbura on 25 July 1959. He is buried in Mwima.

3.   Mwami Kigeri V (Prince Jean Ntahindurwa) succeeded his half-brother in 1959. In 1960 he was deposed by the Belgian colonial administration in favor of an ethnic Abahutu. He went into exile, first in Uganda and then settled in Nairobi. He was employed as a government clerk before becoming a king.

4.   Gregoire Kayibanda was born in Rwanda to Hutu peasants. He attended local primary schools and later a Catholic seminary to study for the priesthood. He left the seminary and was employed by a Belgian bishop as a private secretary. By 1960 Kayibanda was a leading personality in the PARMEHUTU political party. He was elected president after the UN supervised Rwanda's 1961 elections. Though married to a Tutsi woman, Kayibanda presided over the massacre of the Tutsi ethnic group. Kayibanda, in an apparent state of drunkenness, was overthrown in a 1973 military coup led by General Juvenal Havyarimana, then a Chief of the Army.

5.   Approximately thirty thousand Tutsis were massacred between 1959 and 1966. Approximately five hundred thousand Tutsis found

refuge in Burundi, Uganda, Tanzania, and the Democratic Republic of the Congo (Zaire).

6.   Yoweri Museveni is a descendant of the Abahima of Ankole, a distant cousin of the Abatutsi of both Burundi and Rwanda. A former defense minister under President Milton Obote, Museveni led guerrilla bush wars against President Idi Amin, and later against President Obote himself. During the war and thereafter, Museveni's trusted officers were descendants of Rwanda's Tutsi ethnic groups, including Frederick Rwigyema and Paul Kagame, who later led a guerrilla army in Rwanda.

7.   Inkotanyi is translated from Kinyarwanda to mean *indefatigable ones*. The names Inkotanyi and Rwandan Patriotic Front (RPF) are used interchangeably in this text.

8.   The Inkotanyi reported that General Frederick Rwigyema was killed in battle but rumors persisted that he was actually killed by his deputy, Peter Bayingana, over war efforts tactics. General Rwigyema is said to have preferred a gradual approach in military tactics while Bayingana preferred a comprehensive blitzkrieg up to Kigali. Within two weeks of General Rwigyema's death, Bayingana was also mysteriously killed.

9.   Paul Kagame was born in Inyundo, Rwanda. His parents fled to Uganda when he was two years old. He grew up in a refugee camp. After high school he and Frederick Rwigyema joined in Yoweri Museveni's bush wars against Ugandan despots Idi Amin and Milton Obote. Upon Museveni's victory Kagame rose to become Chief of the Ugandan Military Intelligence. In 1990 he attended the United States Army Command and Staff College in Fort Leavenworth, Kansas. Upon the death of Rwigyema, Kagame was appointed Supreme Commander of the RPF army. Tall and thin, Kagame is a typical representative of Rwanda's Tutsi physical features and perhaps one of the few of his ethnic group who embodies the traditional Tutsi virtues. A brilliant military strategist, tactician, and disciplinarian, Kagame led RPF guerrilla forces to victory against Rwanda's regular army in July 1994. He now serves as Vice-President and Minister of Defense in Rwanda.

10.   There are approximately nine thousand French legionnaires in Africa. They can be found in Central African Republic, Chad, the Ivory Coast, Djibouti, Gabon, Reunion, Rwanda, and Senegal. Fifteen thousand paratroopers are maintained in southern France, ready to intervene in any French-speaking African nation within twenty-four hours. Since the early 1960s, France has intervened in Senegal (1962), Gabon (1964, 1990), Chad (1968, 1978, 1983, 1986), Zaire (1977, 1978), Central African Republic (1979), Togo (1986), Comoros Islands (1979), and Rwanda (1994).

11.   The main points of the Arusha Peace Accords include: (a) return of refugees, (b) abolition of identity cards, (c) a permanent Human Rights Commission, (d) sharing power and fusion of the two armies, (e) establishment of a transitional government leading to free and fair elections, and (f) a neutral international force to provide security.

12.   Approximately 300 thousand Burundian Hutus fled to Rwanda, and 900 thousand Rwandan Hutus were displaced by the Rwandan Patriotic Front (RPF).

13.   Prime Minister Agathe Uwilingiyimana was dragged out of a guarded United Nations (UN) compound and slashed to death with a machete. Killed in the same manner were several of her cabinet ministers and the president of the Supreme Court, Joseph Kavaruganda. Upon surrendering their arms, UN Belgian peacekeepers had their tendons, eyes, and noses cut off before the final *coup de grace*. The new prime minister, Faustin Twagirarnungu, was first on the hit list, though they missed him by pure chance. He escaped to Nairobi, and then to Brussels.

14.   It is estimated that approximately a half-million—almost half of the entire Tutsi population—were massacred within three months. More than one and a half million Rwandans were left homeless, and three million fled to neighboring Burundi, Uganda, Tanzania, and the Democratic Republic of the Congo (Zaire).

15.   Out of a population of eight million, approximately three million Hutu fled the country to neighboring Tanzania and the Democratic Republic of the Congo (Zaire). A half million ethnic Tutsi were massacred by the Hutu army and militia.

16.   Approximately 100 thousand Tutsis returned from Uganda with 130 thousand cattle. Eighty thousand returned from Burundi.

17.   Melchior Ndadaye was born in 1953 in Inyabihanga, Muramvya Province. He attended primary school in Kibumbu and secondary school in Kitega. During the inter-ethnic conflict of 1972 he fled to Rwanda, spending his adult life in refugee camps. He returned to Burundi under refugee amnesty and found a job at Banque Meridien in charge of credit. He organized the *Front pour la democracy au Burundi* (FRODEBU) political party, which was a domestic branch of an exclusively racist *Parti pour la liberation du peuple Hutu* (PALIPEHUTU). PALIPEHUTU was operated from the outside and financed by neo-colonial interests. Ndadaye won the elections on 1 June 1993, only to be assassinated on 21 October 1993.

18.   Emile Durkheim, a noted anthropologist, defines animism as a belief in cosmic things—such as wind, rivers, stars, sky, plants, animals, and rocks. Animism is a belief in spirits, souls, geniuses, demons, and divinities that are not ordinarily visible to human eyes.

19.   Imana is also referred to as Rurema, Rugiravyose, Sengovyi, Nyenijuru, Sebibondo, Incanyi, Indavyi, and Dah wa twese.

20.   Gihanga is found in Burundi folklore. Certain popular names, nouns, and verbs are patterned after him—*Ruhangare* is a person's proper name, *Igihanga* is a name of a town in Bubanza Province, *guhanga* is to be disrespectful, and *uruhanga* is the forehead.

21.   The Abatwa are cousins of the Ababo, Abaragane, and Abamoso. They are the distant cousins of the Bambuti of the Congo and the Bushmen of the Kalahari Desert. They may also be *australopithecus aforensis* (the original hominids), the ancestors of mankind. These freedom-loving people truly believe and practice democracy. They even decided on equal body sizes for their members. Their hunting and dancing techniques are unique, and their melodic language deserves linguistic research. The Abahutu migrated to Burundi from Tanzania and the area now known as the Democratic Republic of the Congo. Skillful in soil science, they grow a variety of fruits, vegetables, and grains. Certain Abahutu are diviners with magical powers that can cause rain to fall and seeds to germinate. They can protect crops from insects and cattle from diseases. The Abatutsi

entered the area from the region that is present day Ethiopia and Somalia. Like their distant cousins, the Oromos and Gallas, Abatutsis are essentially nomadic pastoralists.

22.   In Burundi, Abahima refers to the descendants of Ham. According to biblical myth, God cursed Canaan, the son of Ham, and his descendants to be "the hewers of wood and the drawers of water" (Joshua 9:23-27). The Calvinistic theory of predestination draws its inspiration from this myth. Another biblical legend tells us Noah had instructed his sons (Shem, Ham, and Japheth) and their wives to abstain from sexual intercourse while in the ark. Ham disregarded his father's instructions and had sex with his wife. Out of this union a son, Cush, was born. Noah cursed Ham and his descendants to be loathsome and servants of servants. Cush became the ancestor of the Cushites (Blacks). Blacks were burdened with a black heart, black skin, and to be servants of the descendants of Shem and Japheth. In South Africa, *Afrikaners* justified apartheid on the basis that God chose them for salvation while *Africans* were chosen for servitude. Still a third version of this myth is found in the Babylonian Talmud (second to sixth century A.D.). After the flood, Noah was found in a state of drunkenness by Ham, his second son. Instead of covering him, Ham went back to the fields and told his brothers. Shem and Japheth went to the tent and covered their father. When Noah awoke he cursed Ham and blessed his brothers.

23.   The Abapfasoni were clans of nobility, either as direct descendants from the royal clan or through marriage. Some traditional clans of nobility included Abaterwa, Abashoka, Abanyakarama, Abenengwe, Ababibe, Abasapfu, Abanyarwanda, and Abahondogo. Each clan was organized around a political-spiritual leader who had a psychological impact on its members. Clannish descent was always traced through the patrilineal system. Abatare and Abezi ruling clans maintain political hegemony in the present day Tanzania; Abanyamwezi and Abatare are dominant across the Muragarazi river in Tanzania.

24.   Mwami Ntare Rushatsi Cambarantama was born in Buha in 1500 B.C. A skillful military strategist, Mwami Cambarantama crossed the Muragarazi River with his army and proceeded to overthrow the

local chieftains, including Ruhanga, Fumbije, Jabwe, and Ruhnda. By the time of his death, he had established himself as the uncontested Mwami of Burundi. His unbroken dynasty continued until the overthrow of Mwami Ntare V in November 1966.

25.   The reader should not confuse *Umuhutu* (pl. Abahutu) which refers to the anthropological ethnic grouping of the Bantuoid African group, and *umuhutu* (pl. abahutu) which in feudal jargon refers to a serf in relationship to his *shebuja* or *databuja* (lord).

26.   Although Mwami Mwambutsa IV Bangiricenge refused to be baptized or recognize any authority above his, all of his *abaganwa* and *abatware* sported Christian names as a badge of qualification. Mwami Mwambutsa IV acquiesced to marry a newly converted Catholic girl, Therese Kanyonga, of the Abasine clan. His children were forced to be baptized in a Catholic church. His remarriage to Baramparaye had to be approved by the Pope. Catholic hierarchy played an important role in the nomination of *abaganwa* and *abatware*. Traditional rulers who resisted Catholicism were summarily dismissed at the instigation of a local priest. As an example, Umuganwa Nteturuye in Nkoma was replaced by Raphael Ndenzako (from the Ruyigi region), and Umuganwa Mukura was replaced by Jean Kigoma (from the Gitega region).

27.   Thirty-four army officers were executed by firing squad at Rwagasore Stadium. Among the political leaders executed were Gervais Nyangoma, Sylvestre Karibwami (the older brother of Nyangoma and President of the Senate), Emile Bucumi (President of the National Assembly), Paul Mirerekano (Vice President of the National Assembly), Joseph Bamina (former Prime Minister), and Paul Ntibirantiza (President of the *Parti du peuple*).

28.   Approximately five hundred Tutsi were massacred in Muramvya Province alone.

29.   Charles Ndizeye was born in Gitega on 1 December 1947, the youngest son of Mwami Mwambutsa IV Bangiricenge and Baramparaye. He attended primary school in Gitega and secondary school in Europe. He enrolled in the University of Lausanne but after failing most of his exams, his father gave him a position in the shaky government of Leopold Bihumugani. Soon thereafter king-makers

and political opportunists persuaded him to depose his aging father. He was crowned Mwami Ntare V on 8 July 1966 and overthrown on 29 November 1966 while attending the first anniversary of Joseph Desiré Mobutu Sese Seko in Kinshasa. He joined his father in exile in Europe. By bizarre circumstances, Mwami Ntare V appeared in Kampala, Uganda, in March 1972. With President Idi Amin's complicity, Mwami Ntare V was thrown to Burundi and executed during a night of uprising on 30 April 1972 in Gitega. Mwami Ntare V was unceremoniously buried with criminals in a common mass grave in Knyambeho near the Catholic Mission of Giheta. With the death of Mwami Ntare V came the end to a five-century-old monarchy.

30.   Louis Rwagasore was born in Gitega on 10 January 1932, the eldest son of Mwami Mwambutsa IV Bangiricenge and Therese Kanyonga. He attended primary school at the Catholic Mission of Mubukeye, Ikanymya, and Igitega. He attended *Group scolaire d'Astrida* in Rwanda and *Ecole coloniale* in Belgium. Unable to finish his studies, he returned to Burundi and was appointed Umuganwa of Ibutanyerera in the territory of Ngozi, succeeding his great uncle Nduwumwe. In 1959 the Belgian colonial administration abolished the institution of *ganwa*ship *(abaganwa)* and *tware*ship *(abatware).* As the wind of independence blew throughout the continent, Prince Rwagasore founded *Union et progres nationale* (UPRONA), which won by an overwhelming majority in the 1961 United Nations (UN) supervised elections. Prince Rwagasore was officially designated Prime Minister. On 13 October 1961 Prince Rwagasore was assassinated while dining with his newly appointed cabinet at the Hotel Tanganyika. Prince Rwagasore, like his great-grandfather Mwami Mwezi Gisabo, had violated two important Burundi traditional taboos: never to eat in public and never to face the waters of Lake Tanganyika.

31.   Lemarchand, Réné. "The Hutu-Tutsi Conflict in Burundi," *Genocide and Human Rights.*

32.   Michel Micombero was born in Rutovu to Ruronona, a member of an impoverished Abahima family. He attended primary school in Rutovu and secondary school at *College du St. Esprit,* a Jesuit-run institution in Bujumbura. Upon graduation he enrolled in the Military Academy in Brussels. Unable to finish his studies, he returned to

Burundi to be appointed Secretary of Defense in the infant Burundi army. Mwami Ntare V appointed Micombero to the post of Prime Minister in 1966. Three months later Micombero proclaimed himself President of the First Republic. The leading coup plotters were Major Albert Shibura and Sylvere Sota. Micombero was overthrown in 1976 while in a state of drunkenness. He died in Somalia.

33.   Among the prominent personalities executed were Minister of Planning Bamabe Kanyaruguru and the First Secretary of the Burundi Embassy in Washington D.C., Gregoire Nicimbikije.

34.   Among the accused were Minister of Information Major Jerome Ntungumburanye; Foreign Ministers Marc Manirakiza, Lazare Nhwurishira, and Libere Ndabakwaje; and the Ambassador to France, Charles Baranyanka (a younger brother of Umuganwa Ntidendereza and Joseph Birori).

35.   Forty Tutsi government officials were murdered. Two thousand Tutsi were killed.

36.   Marc Ndayiziga was born in Musema, Ngozi Province, to Dawudi Nkurikiyo, an influential Baptist pastor. He attended the local primary school in Musema and was admitted to the prestigious *Ecole prepetoire de Muyebe*. Because the schools were segregated along religious affiliations Muyebe attracted gifted sixth grade Protestant children from both Rwanda and Burundi. After graduation, Marc Ndayiziga was admitted to *Groupe scolaire d'Astrida,* a rare occurrence for Protestant students. There, the young Ndayiziga met two more Protestant students from Matana: Gorvais Nyangoma and Albert Shibura. They lived together, Protestants among a sea of Catholic students. Later, they distinguished themselves in Burundian politics. In 1960 Ndayiziga was admitted to *Universite libre de Bruxelles,* where he graduated with a degree in Engineering. Upon his return to Burundi he was appointed Minister of Public Works. During the 1972 Tutsi massacre, Ndayiziga was at the World Bank on an official mission with Minister of Finance Joseph Hicuburundi. I met with Ndayiziga before he returned to Burundi. We talked about the political conditions in Burundi. As the Abarundi always like to summarize their thoughts in proverbial statements, he said, "Mon cher Nyankanzi, les chiens aboient et la caravane passe" (My dear

friend Nyankanzi, the dogs bark but the caravan passes). He was alluding to Hutu-Tutsi political tensions. While in transit with Hicuburundi at Brussels Airport, they heard reports of heavy fighting back home. Hicuburundi convinced Ndayiziga to fly back to Bujumbura with him. Upon his arrival at Bujumbura Airport Ndayiziga was kidnapped in a beaten-up Volkswagon. His young brother, Silas Niyonzima, a history professor in Kibimba, and his older sister Monique Nzikobanyanka, the director of *Corporation/Radio de l'Afrique Centrale* (CORDAC) also met similar fates.

37.   Ten thousand ethnic Tutsi and 150 thousand ethnic Hutu were killed in 1972.

38.   The 1976 leading coup leaders were: Lieutenant Colonel Jean-Baptiste Bagaza, who became President of the Second Republic; Lieutenant Colonel Edouard Nzambimana, who became Prime Minister and then Minister of Foreign Affairs; Sylvere Nzohabonayo, who became *Administrateur de la Surete;* and Lieutenant Colonel Gabriel Ndikumana, who became Minister of the Interior. However, the group soon disintegrated and Bagaza emerged triumphant.

39.   Jean-Baptiste Bagaza was born in Murambi in 1946. He attended primary school in Rutovu and secondary school at *College du St. Esprit* in Bujumbura. He enrolled at the *Ecole royale des cadets* in Brussels. Upon his return to Burundi, he was appointed Deputy Chief of Staff by President Micombero. After the coup in 1976 Bagaza became President of the Second Republic. President Bagaza was overthrown in 1987 and remained in exile in Libya until 1993. He currently lives quietly in Bujumbura.

40.   Isidore Nyaboya was born into the Abayanzi clan in Kumugano, Bururi Province. He attended a local primary school in Kumugano and Murumeza. He enrolled at the *College du St. Esprit* in Bujumbura. After graduation he won a scholarship to study in the United States. He enrolled first in the English Language program at the University of Kansas at Lawrence, and then transferred to New York University. As we were the first few Burundi students to study in metropolitan New York, Nyaboya and I spent most of our free time together, either partying with other international students or in the association of African diplomats at the United Nations (UN). Upon

graduation we were employed at the UN Secretariat in New York. In 1976 he was appointed Minister of Public Works and Energy by President Bagaza but gradually functioned as a de facto Prime Minister. After the overthrow of President Bagaza in 1987, Prime Minister Nyaboya was accused of embezzling public funds. He was imprisoned until 1993. Today he lives quietly in Brussels.

41.   Pierre Buyoya was born in Kumutangaro, Bururi Province. He attended primary and secondary school in Rutovu. He was admitted to the Military Academy in Brussels. Upon his return he was appointed Commander of the prestigious Camp Muha. After the overthrow of President Jean-Baptiste Bagaza he became President of the Third Republic. Buyoya was defeated in the first presidential elections in 1993. At this writing he lives quietly in Bujumbura.

42.   In 1988 five hundred ethnic Tutsi and twenty thousand ethnic Hutu were killed. Thousands were maimed and thousands more fled to Rwanda, Tanganyika, and the Democratic Republic of the Congo (Zaire).

43.   "Le Corbeau et le Renard," *Les Fables de LaFontaine*.

44.   President Melchior Ndadaye spoke to the United Nations (UN) General Assembly on 4 October 1993. The same evening, President Ndadaye was received by *la Communaute Burundaise* at the New York Plaza Hotel. The following day he left for an official visit to Washington D.C.

45.   Inyabihanga is the native region of President Melchior Ndadaye.

46.   Mwanzari is the native region of President of the National Assembly Pontien Karibwami, and Gishubi is the native region of President Sylvestre Ntibantunganya.

47.   The most effected villages in Rutana Province included Kumpinga, Ibutambara, Kumuyogoro, Kumunyika, Mugitwa, Mugasasa, Ibutimbo, Mukiguhu, Inyakazu, Ikibinzi, Inyakabanda, and Injhinga.

48.   Cyprien Ntaryamira was born in Mubimbi. Like the rest of the *Front pour la democracy au Burundi* (FRODEBU) core leadership, Ntaryamira spent most of his adult years in refugee camps in Rwanda. After the 1993 elections, Ntaryamira was appointed Minister of

Agriculture. Upon Ndadaye's assassination, Ntaryamira was selected to be the interim president by the FRODEBU-dominated
parliament. President Ntaryamira died in a mysterious plane crash on
6 April 1994 with President Havyarimana of Rwanda.

49.   Sylvestre Ntibantunganya was born in Inyabiraba, Kitega Province. During the 1972 abortive Tutsi massacre he fled to Rwanda
where he spent most of his adult life in refugee camps. He returned
to Burundi under refugee amnesty and was one of the founders of the
Front pour la democracy au Burundi (FRODEBU), a domestic arm
of *Parti pour la liberation du peuple Hutu* (PALIPEHUTU), an
extremist mono-ethnic political party. FRODEBU received funds
and strategic planning from Belgian-French neo-colonial interests.
FRODEBU's intended objective was the extermination of ethnic
Tutsi. Its ideology is linked to the 1959 Rwandan *Parti pour
l'emancipation Hutu* (PARMEHUTU). Its patron saint was Juvenal
Havyarimana of Rwanda. Under President Melchior Ndadaye,
Ntibantunganya became Foreign Minister. After President Ndadaye's
assassination he became the Speaker of the Parliament. Upon the
untimely death of President Ntaryamira, Ntibantunganya inherited
the presidency. He was overthrown in a peaceful *coup d'état* on
25 July 1996. His presidency will be remembered in the dark
pages of Burundi history. As an anonymous young lady commented,
"Ntibantunganya was the president of Hutu thieves."
Ntibantunganya is responsible for the Tutsi genocide of 1993. As
such, he should be tried for the crimes against humanity under
Articles II and III alienas (b), (c), (d), and (e) of the United
Nations (UN) Convention on the Prevention and Punishment of
the Crime of Genocide.

50.   Leonard Nyangoma was born in Murumeza, Bururi Province.
He studied mathematics, but like his namesake Gervais Nyangoma,
Leonard is better known for his extremist ethnic Hutu views. During
Melchior Ndadaye's regime he was appointed Minister of Labor, a
position he used to fire every Tutsi civil servant. Upon Ndadaye's
assassination, from Radio/Kigali, he called for the dismantling of the
Burundi army. In Sylvestre Ntibantunganya's government Leonard
Nyangoma was appointed Minister of the Interior, a position he used
to recruit Hutu squads. He then fled to Europe. Shortly thereafter he

surfaced in Kivu, Democratic Republic of the Congo (Zaire) with a genocidal plan exhorting every Hutu to kill at least one Tutsi. Since then, Hutu genocidal squads under the aegis of the National Council of the Defense of Democracy (CNDD) had conducted a hit-and-run guerrilla war. Leonard received funds from Western Europe and logistics from Joseph Desiré Mobutu Sese Seko.

51. *New York Times*, 25 July 1996.

52. Between the attempted Tutsi genocide of October 1993 and the peaceful coup of July 1996 that ended Sylvestre Ntibantunganya's presidency, 150,000 people were slaughtered. The attempted Tutsi genocide alone claimed 50,000 lives and 2,100 civilians were killed in subsequent attacks. Eight hundred people perished in Kivyuka; 500 lost their lives in Ayeshenza, Cibitoke Province; 500 were killed in Buhoro. At the administrative center of Bugendana, 40 ethnic Tutsi were massacred. One week later, 30 more were killed in Mucibitoke. The presence of more than 150,000 Rwandan Hutu refugees in Burundi and 100,000 internally displaced residents further complicated Burundi's political landscape.

53. *New York Times*, 24 July 1996.

54. *New York Times*, 26 July 1996.

55. The Organization of African Unity (OAU) committee included: Cameroon, Ethiopia, Kenya, Rwanda, Uganda, Tanzania, and the Democratic Republic of the Congo (Zaire).

56. Julius Kamparage Nyerere was born in Musoma in the British Tanganyika Trust Territory. He attended local Catholic schools and Makerere College. He received a Master's degree in History in England. In the 1950s and early 1960s, Nyerere led the country to independence. Nyerere's political activity contributed substantially to African leadership and statesmanship both nationally and internationally. He successfully intervened in the Zanzibari revolution and on the island of Sechelles. He ended the bloody Idi Amin dictatorship in Uganda. His country became the backbone of southern Africa's liberation movements. With the exception of Senghor of Senegal, he peacefully passed the torch to new Tanzanian leadership. But his recent support of an economic embargo and multinational intervention in Burundi is a

departure from his past policies. He has lent his voice of reason to a poor cause. Inter-ethnic peaceful negotiations are still possible.

57.   Chad, Malawi, Uganda, Tanzania, and Zambia agreed to contribute troops. The United States agreed to provide transportation, communications, and logistics. But multinational military intervention never achieves its intended objectives. It failed in Congo, Somalia, Liberia, Rwanda, and even in Bosnia.

58.   Burundi, a landlocked country, has its imports and exports processed at the ports of Dar-Salaam and Kigoma, Tanzania, and at the port of Mombasa in Kenya. But an economic embargo never achieves its intended objectives.

59.   Mwami Ntare Ndizeye was executed in Kitega during the abortive coup of 1972. President Melchior Ndadaye was executed in an attempted coup in 1993. President Cyprien Ntaryamira was killed in a suspicious airplane crash along with Rwandan President Juvenal Havyarimana. Surviving Burundians included Bagaza, Buyoya, and Sylvestre Ntibantunganya. Mwami Mwambutsa, who barely escaped assassination during the abortive coup of 1965, died in exile in Switzerland. President Micombero died in exile in Somalia. Prince Louis Rwagasore, then Prime Minister designate, was assassinated in 1961 while dining with his cabinet at Hotel Tanganyika. Prime Minister Ngendandumwe (Hutu) was assassinated in 1963 while visiting his wife at Clinic Rwagasore. Prime Minister Leopold Bihumugani was shot and seriously wounded during the abortive coup of 1965. Prime Minister Bamina was executed as a result of reprisal for the Hutu attempted coup in 1965. The lucky surviving Prime Ministers include: Andre Muhirwa, Albin Nyamoya, Adrien Sibomana (recently escaped attempted assassination), Kinigi (first woman to become Prime Minister), Kanyenkiko, Nduwayo, and Ndimira (recently appointed by President Buyoya).

60.   Other German colonies in Africa were Cameroon, Togoland, and southwest Africa (Namibia). After Germany was defeated in the First World War its former colonies were administered as Society of Nations mandates. After the Second World War they were converted into United Nations (UN) trusteeship territories.

61. Mwami Mwezi Gisabo (1830-1908) was the youngest and favorite son of Mwami Ntue Tutanganwa. He ascended to the Burundi throne in 1852 upon the death of his father. In his early years he lost sight in one eye and was paralyzed in one leg. His principal royal residence was in Muramvya, where he spent most of his time. His other royal residences were in Ikiganda and Mubukeye. Mwami Gisabo died on 21 August 1908.

62. Mwami Mwezi Gisabo's rivals included Kilima, Maconco, Kanugunu (grandfather of Andre Muhirwa, the first Prime Minister of independent Burundi), Busokoza, and Rusengo.

63. Mwami Mwambutsa IV Bangiricenge's trusted advisers were: Germain Bimpenda, his cousin and *Grand marechal a la cour;* Léopold Bihumugani, his cousin, Private Secretary, and Prime Minister in 1965; Andre Muhirwa, his son-in-law and the first Prime Minister in 1962; and Leon Ndenzako, his son-in-law and the first Ambassador to the United States.

64. Eighty-five percent of Burundi's exports and imports pass through the ports of Dar-es-Salaam and Kigoma.

65. In the early 1930s American Protestant missions began active evangelization in Burundi. They included: the Friends Gospel Mission (Kibimba, Mutaho, Kwibuka, and Kwisumo), Free Methodist Mission (Muyebe, Rwintare, and Kibuye), World Gospel Mission (Kayero, Murore, and Murehe), a joint-venture Bible School (Mweya), and a hospital to treat leprosy (Nyenkanda). Other European-sponsored Protestant missions in Burundi included the Church Mission Society (Matana, Buye, and Buhiga), Danish Baptist Mission (Musema and Rubura), and the Mission Pentecostale Suedoise (Bujumbura and Kiremba). Together they formed the *Alliance Protestante du Ruanda-Urundi.*

66. Joseph Desiré Mobutu Sese Seko (1930–) was born in Lisala, Equator Province. He attended Catholic schools in Coquilathville. Afterwards he spent a year at *Institut d'Etudes Sociales* in Brussels. Upon his return to the Congo, he joined *Mouvement nationale Congolais* (MNC). After independence Prime Minister Lumumba gave Mobutu the position of commander of the infant *Force publique*

(Congo's army). In his quest for African authenticity, President Mobutu changed his name from Joseph Desiré Mobutu to Mobutu Sese Seko Kuku Ngebendu Wa Za Banga (all-powerful warrior who will go from conquest to conquest, leaving fire in his wake). He also changed the name of the country from Congo to Zaire. Mobutu's symbols of authority included the leopard (predatory cunning) and eagle (serene ability to hover above mortals below). Although Mobutu's hidden Swiss accounts are estimated at five billion dollars, the extent of his total fortune is unknown. He is reported to own a thirty-room mansion in Savigny, Switzerland, and a villa in the French Riviera. His villa at Cote d' Azur, purchased from a Saudi billionaire, has been described as a "symbol of absolute power." Overlooking Monaco, the villa is surrounded by pet sheep, lemon trees, and elaborate floral arrangements. Mobutu's other assets are reported to be in Austria, Portugal, Spain, and the United States. In his native village, Gabdolite, his marble palace is patrolled by a fleet of peacocks. The Western Press has depicted Mobutu as a dictator who "bled his country to the bone." In France he has been satirically portrayed as a walking bank balance with a leopard-skin hat.

67.   During the scramble for Africa at the Berlin Conference in 1884-85, King Leopold acquired a vast territory that he named Congo Free State. He plundered its natural resources and nearly enslaved its inhabitants. Those who could not meet the quotas had their limbs cut off.

68.   Monkey is the Democratic Republic of the Congo's (Zaire) national delicacy.

69.   The Democratic Republic of the Congo's (Zaire) natural resources include sixty percent of the world's cobalt, industrial diamonds, zinc, copper, manganese, gold, ivory, rubber, and timber.

70.   Laurent Kabila is an ethnic Muluba of Shaba (Katanga). He was trained in guerrilla warfare under Ernesto Che Guevara. In the early 1960s he fought in the Simba rebellion. In the 1970s he fought with the Katanga rebels. Kabila befriended Yoweri Museveni and Paul Kagame during their bush wars against dictators Idi Amin and Milton Obote. Most of Kabila's senior officers are drawn from the ethnic Tutsi of Burundi, Rwanda, and Uganda. After the collapse of

the 1970s insurrections, Kabila, along with a band of his follow-ers, spent the last twenty years in exile or underground. They survived by mining gold in the Fizi-Baraka mountains.

71.   *Guardian*, 2 November 1966.

72.   Hutu refugee Camps in the Democratic Republic of the Congo (Zaire): Mugunga Camp had 400,000 Hutu refugees, out of which 40,000 were former Rwandan Hutu soldiers and 10,000 were former members of the Hutu militia (Interahamwe); Goma Refugee Camp had 300,000 Hutu refugees; Bukavu Refugee Camp had 500,000 Hutu refugees; and Uvira Refugee Camp had 500,000 refugees, out of which 143,000 refugees were from Burundi.

73.   Kengo Wa Dongo's mother is of Rwandan Tutsi descent. His father is of Polish descent (in a patriarchal society, like that of the ethnic Tutsi, the father's side is more emphasized than the mother's). *Le Potentiel,* 1 November 1996.

74.   *New York Times*, 17 November 1996. *Guardian*, 2 Novem-ber 1996.

75.   Yoweri Museveni was born to ethnic Tutsi (Abahima) in Ankole, Uganda. Ankole was then ruled by *umukama* (kings). Museveni helped Milton Obote oust Idi Amin and then commanded a bush guerrilla war against Obote. Museveni became President of Uganda in 1987.

76.   The countries of the Great Lakes region include Burundi, Rwanda, Uganda, and the Democratic Republic of the Congo (Zaire).

77.   In 1898 General Marchand's French military expedition con-fronted General Kitchener's British military expedition in Fashoda (Sudan). General Kitchener threatened to use force if *les europeans quelconques* under Marchand resisted. After Anglo-French diplo-matic maneuvers, war was avoided. A humiliated French expedition finally withdrew from Fashoda. Similarly, this time by proxy, a humiliated France withdrew from Rwanda.

78.   Canada's Ambassador to the United States, Raymond Chretien (a nephew of the Prime Minister of Canada) was appointed by the United Nations (UN) to negotiate a cease-fire in the Democratic Republic of the Congo (Zaire). Canadian General Maurice Basil was

appointed Commander of the UN International Force in the Democratic Republic of the Congo (Zaire). Canada pledged 1,500 troops and $11,300,000. They dispatched 34 advance reconnaissance teams and Hercules transport planes to Kigali, Rwanda. Likewise, the United States government pledged 4,000 troops, out of which 1,000 were stationed in the Democratic Republic of the Congo (Zaire) and 3,000 in nearby Kenya and Uganda. Eight hundred soldiers were dispatched from the 1st Battalion and 508th Airforce Infantry based in Vicenza, Italy. The United States government also pledged logistical navy supplies and $140,000,000. According to military plans, Entebbe, Nairobi and Kigali Airports would serve as staging bases while Goma and Bukavu would serve as forward bases.

79.   More than thirty-five hundred United States, Belgian, and French troops (including fifteen hundred United States marines) had been stationed in Congo/Brazzaville across the Congo River from Kinshasa and Gabon in readiness for evacuation of their nationals in case things got out of hand.

80.   *New York Times*, 29 April 1997.

81.   Melos was an Island in the Aegean Sea, southeast of the Greek mainland. During the Peloponnesian Wars, Melos was important for its strategic position as well as for manufacturing weapons.

82.   Thucydides. *History of the Peloponnesian War.*

83.   In Auschwitz alone, 1,000,000 Jews perished. Eight hundred thousand were killed in Treblinka; 250,000 in Sobibor; 150,000 in Kulnihof; and 10,000 in Lublin. Two hundred and fifty thousand Gypsies met their fate in the crematoria.

84.   By the end of 1915, one million Armenians had been massacred by Ottoman agents.

85.   Christopher Columbus was born in 1451 in Genoa, Italy. Columbus was a sailer. When his ship wrecked near Lisbon, Portugal, he remained there to join various expeditions to the African coast, the South Atlantic, and Iceland. Portugal, a small maritime power, was interested in finding a trade route to the Orient, especially in search of spices which were needed to preserve meat during the winter. A bag of pepper was worth a man's life. Gold and silver were

the most valuable metals. Columbus, by then an experienced sailor, proposed an alternate westward route to Asia because the Ottoman authorities in Constantinople had closed trade routes to European powers in its empire. After a lengthy debate, King Ferdinand and Queen Isabella of Spain finally agreed to finance Columbus' explorations in 1492. On 3 August 1492, Columbus, with a crew which included some Africans, left the port of Polos in three ships: the Pinta, the Niña, and the Santa Maria. Instead of heading east, the winds pushed them westward. They first landed in the Bahamas, which they thought was Zipango (Japan), then the island of Santo Domingo (today's Haiti and Dominican Republic), which Columbus baptized Hispaniola. Its inhabitants, Caribes and Tainos, were mistakenly called Indians (the name has stayed with them to this day). When he returned to Spain he brought gold, tobacco, and Indian captives. But to the chagrin of Queen Isabella, there were no spices. He was given the title of Governor of Hispaniola by the Spanish Crown. During subsequent voyages he discovered Puerto Rico, Jamaica, Trinidad, and Venezuela. But the newly appointed Governor of Hispaniola arrested Columbus and returned the poor prisoner in chains to Spain where he died penniless in 1506, still convinced that he had discovered India.

86.   The estimated population was 35,000,000 in pre-Colombian Mexico; 35,000,000 in the Andean region; and 13,000,000 in Central America. The Aztecs, Incas, and Mayas totaled 70,000,000-90,000,000. A century later they were reduced to a mere 3,500,000.

87.   Galeano, Edourdo. *Open Veins*.

88.   Fort Dimanche prison in Port-au-Prince is a symbol of genocide to the Haitian people. Built in 1920, it became a center of death camps and torture for what the Haitian government considered "enemies of state." The accused men were beaten, electrocuted, dismembered, blinded, and castrated, while others were starved to death. The torturers under the Douvalier regime were the most feared Tontons Macoutes. After Douvalier, they were baptized attachés (paramilitary thugs).

89.   From 1600 to the 1890 massacre at Wounded Knee, ninety-nine percent of the North American Indian population had been wiped out.

90.   In 1641 Massachusetts passed a series of laws for the purpose of establishing perpetual enslavement of the people of African descent. Blacks were not allowed to own property or weapons, testify before the courts, vote, hold office, or educate their own offspring in Virginia or Maryland. The Louisiana Slave Code stated that "the slave can do nothing, possess nothing, acquire nothing, but what must belong to his master." Slaves were sold on the open market, bred like cattle, gambled at poker tables, deeded in wills, and presented as gifts at social events. It was a crime to teach a slave how to read and write. Other states passed similar Black Codes, some of which included vagrancy, property, and apprenticeship laws. Slavery was designed to turn human beings into human machines. The underlying motive was economic exploitation, while racism was conveniently used to justify Black labor. After the abolition of the slave trade, interstate slave trading became a major source of income. A field hand netted $1,800 and a blacksmith $2,500. A beautiful mulatto girl could be sold for $5,000 to be used as a house servant as well as for the sexual pleasure of the master. By 1860 miscegenation accounted for twenty percent of the Black population. Three-fourths of the United States Black population claimed White ancestry in 1976. The 1868 Plessy v. Ferguson case sanctioned the doctrine of "separate but equal" until the landmark case of Brown vs. The Board of Education in 1954. The 1957 Dred Scott case implied that Blacks had no rights that Whites needed to respect. Blacks in America were considered things— animals—pieces of property to be bought and sold, used and abused. In the American Constitution, a Black man was considered to be less than human and was defined as three-fifths of a person.

91.   Pascoe, Elaine. *Racial Prejudice*, Franklin Watts, 1985.

92.   In 1904 there were eighty thousand ethnic Herero in southwest Africa and fourteen thousand ethnic German settlers. By the end of the Herero-German war in 1911, fifteen thousand ethnic Herero had survived.

93.   Similar genocidal activities occurred in Angola, Chad, Equatorial Guinea, Ethiopia, Liberia, Nigeria, Mozambique, Rwanda, Somalia, South Africa, Sudan, and Uganda.

94.   Between 1700 and 1987, over one hundred million people were killed in Europe. The Soviet Union's Communist regime killed over a half million people between 1917 and 1987.

95.   In this context, Africans means Blacks regardless of their geographical location. It also excludes non-Blacks who happened to live in continental Africa, like Whites in South Africa or Arabs in North Africa.

96.   The Hebrew tetragrammaton YHVH (God) is known as Yahveh, Yahweh, Elohim, Adonai (Lord), EL Shaddai (God of the Mountain), EL (High God of Canaan), EL Elyon (God Most High), Eloah, EL Olam (God of Eternity), EL Berith (God of the Convenant), EL Roi (God of Seeing), Jah, Yah, Jehovah, Abba (Father), and Sabaoth (Lord of Hosts). EL appears in Hebrew names such as Isra-el, Ishma-el, Beth-el, etc. EL was worshipped in Syria and his son Balal was considered God of Vegetation and Fertility.

97.   Abraham (in Hebrew, Avraham), meaning *father of a multitude of nations,* was born in Ur, Chaldea (modern Iraq), in 1300 B.C. Like his countrymen, he practiced idolatry. As Abraham and Sarah were getting old and were without child, she decided to give him her Black Egyptian maidservant as a concubine. Out of this union a son, Ishmael, was born. Today, Arabs claim Ishmael to be their ancestor. One day, God sent three angels to inform Abraham and Sarah that she would give birth to a son. When Sarah heard the news she laughed. But Sarah conceived and a son was born. He was called Isaac (laughter). Upon Isaac's birth, Abraham expelled Haggai and their son Ishmael from his household. Perhaps that is why Jews and Arabs are still enemies. Isaac married his cousin, Rebecca, who gave birth to twin sons, Essau and Jacob. Jacob (Israel) also married his two cousins, Rachel and Leah, who gave birth to the twelve sons who became the twelve tribes of Israel. Today Israelites claim Jacob to be their direct ancestor. Abraham is portrayed by Judaism, Christianity, and Islam as a righteous man who reached perfection through the knowledge of the true God. He is considered the father of monotheism. His God became a patron God of his descendants from Isaac, Jacob, and through Jewish prophets up to this day. Abraham and his wife are believed to have been buried in the cave of Machpelah, near Hebron.

98.   Moses (in Hebrew, Mosheh) was born to Levite parents in Egypt in 1300 B.C. His mother, Jochebed, afraid of the Pharaoh's order to kill all newborn Hebrew boys, decided to hide baby Moses in a basket of reeds on the banks of the Nile River. After three months, the infant was discovered by the Pharaoh's daughter, who named him Moses, meaning drawn from water. Moses grew up and received his education at the Pharaoh's royal court. During his adulthood, he began to identify with Hebrews and one day killed an Egyptian overseer who was abusing a Hebrew slave. He fled to Median, a village on the Arabian Peninsula. There he met and married a Black Ethiopian woman, Zipporah. While in Sinai, Moses experienced theophany in the burning bush and was commissioned by Yahweh to lead the Israelites out of Egypt. Moses died at the age of 120 before reaching the promised land. He was succeeded by Joshua. The Israelites remained in the desert for 40 years before the walls of Jericho fell. Moses is credited for writing the Book of Deuteronomy and the God-inspired Ten Commandments. Early Christian church writers portray Moses as the Spirit of Law and the Word of God.

99.   David was born in Bethlehem in 1037 B.C. He was the youngest son of Jesse, born into the tribe of Judah. As a young boy, David tended his father's sheep. A lonely shepherd in the Palestinian desert, David learned to entertain himself with a flute. Later he perfected his musicology by playing a harp. He grew up to become a brave warrior. According to legend, he killed a lion and a bear with his bare hands. He also proved his bravery by slaying the giant, Goliath, with one smooth stone and a sling. For his heroism he was offered the daughter of King Saul, Michah. King Saul suspected David of wanting to usurp the throne and attempted to kill him on several occasions. Upon the death of King Saul, David became the King of Judah for seven years and later was appointed King of all the tribes of Israel. He reigned for forty years. King David is also remembered for his poetic ingenuity. One of his masterpieces, the Book of Psalms, has been quoted throughout history (see Psalms 23).

100.   Mary (Marianne) was a Semitic name given to godmother. The name is a symbol of fertility and healing power. Mary's other divine titles include: Queen of Heaven, Spouse of the Eternal Father,

Blessed Virgin Mary, Mater Dei (Mother of God), Mater Virgo, and Stella Maris (Star of the Sea). According to Catholic legend, the Virgin Mary appeared in Lourdes, France in 1857 and Portugal in 1917. In 1950 thousands of Catholic Converts converged at the Catholic Mission of Mugera waiting for Mary's apparition.

101. The historical Jesus was a revolutionary religio-political figure. He may be compared to modern nationalist leaders such as the reformist Martin Luther, George Washington, Mao-tse-Tung, Fidel Castro, Mahatma Gandhi, Che Guevara, Louis Rwagasore, Patrice Lumumba, Kwame Nkrumah, Julius Nyarere, Nelson Mandela, Fred Rwigyema, Paul Kagame, Marcus Garvey, Martin Luther King, and Malcolm X.

102. The Twelve Disciples were Jews chosen to correspond to the twelve tribes of Israel. They were: Andrew, son of Jona; Philip of Bethsaida; James, son of Zebedee; Bartholomew, son of Tolmai; Simon Peter, son of Jona; John, son of Zebedee; Judas Iscariot, son of Simon; Matthew, son of Alphaeus; Judas (Jude, Thaddeus, Lebacus), son of Joseph; James, son of Alphaeus; Thomas Didynius, the Twin; and Simon the Cananea.

103. In the New Testament Jesus is given the titles: Christos (through whom God is to establish sovereignty), Son of God (the office of the Liberator), Immanuel (God is with us), and Savior (he who brings healing, salvation, and liberation to mankind). His other divine titles include: Lord God, Eternal Life, the Word (Logos), True God, Alpha and Omega, Wonderful, Prince of Peace, Counselor, Almighty God, Son of Man, Bridegroom, Good Shepherd, Light of the World, Son of Righteousness, the Rising Sun, King of Kings, Enlightened One, and the Lion of the Tribe of Judah.

104. Paul was born in 100 A.D., to Jewish parents of Benjamin lineage. He was educated in the traditional Pharisee's legal tradition in Jerusalem, under the great Rabbi Gamaliel. Upon graduation, his first legal assignment was to seek, persecute, and prosecute Christians. It is likely that he witnessed the stoning of Apostle Stephen, the first Christian martyr. On his way to Damascus with a warrant to extradite Christians to Jerusalem for prosecution, Paul was struck by lightning and temporarily lost his sight (Acts 22:7–9). He thought he

was at war with Zeus, the Greek God of Thunder. Through Christian prayers he regained his sight and was instantly converted to Christianity in 33 A.D. It was indeed a turning point in his life. He ceased to practice law and became an Apostle. During his voyages in the Roman Empire, Apostle Paul established Christian centers and performed miracles such as healing the sick, casting out demons, and raising the dead. Like other early Apostles, Paul was arrested several times, stoned, beaten, and thrown in jail. He was finally beheaded in Rome in 67 A.D. His church-related activities are well documented in the Acts of the Apostles as well in his Epistles.

105. King Solomon was a son of King David and Bathsheba. Bathsheba, the wife of Uriah, was a Hittite. Uriah was a descendent of Heth, a son of Canaan (Genesis 10:15, 23:10; 2 Samuel 2; Matthew 1:6). King Solomon is remembered for his wealth and wisdom, as well as his wine and women (according to biblical account he had seven hundred wives and three hundred concubines). One of his wives was a daughter of a Black Egyptian pharaoh.

106. Up to the Edict of Milan in 313 A.D., which recognized freedom of religion, Christians constituted a hated class in the sea of Roman pagans. They were often accused of infanticide, cannibalism, incest, atheism, and mischievous superstition. In the summer of 64 A.D., they were persecuted for allegedly setting a fire which destroyed Rome. Many were put to death. Some were wrapped in animal skins and thrown to dogs before execution. Others were set on fire to illuminate the arena as public entertainment. Under a succession of Roman emperors, thousands of Christians were burned, drowned, thrown into prisons, or exiled. Ironically, Catholic leaders applied similar tactics against their opponents and heretics, especially during the Inquisition.

107. Charles Darwin was born on 12 February 1809 into a family of respected physicians. Upon completion of secondary school in Shresbury, he studied medicine at Edinburgh and later transferred to Cambridge University where he received his B.A. in 1831. While in college he developed a habit of hunting and collecting beetles. Soon after graduation he joined the British naval ship, H.M.S. Beagle, on an expedition to South America as a naturalist. He spent four years

collecting and observing insects, birds, plants, and fossils as far as the Galapagos Islands. While in South America he collected tortoises, snails, and other marine organisms previously unknown. Upon his return to England he continued to study geology, economics, statistics, and biology. He was influenced by Thomas Malthus' Essay on Population. Darwin published *The Origin of Species* in 1859 and *The Descent Of Man* in 1871. His critics point out that some of the variations Darwin discussed were acquired characteristics and that he failed to explain how the variations arose. Nevertheless, his scientific theory of natural selection is ranked alongside Newton's scientific theory of gravity and Einstein's scientific theory of relativity.

108. In early Greco-Roman culture, an Ethiopian (or Black) was described in Latin as *niger, ater, aquilus, exustus, perustus, fucus, percoctus,* and *nocticolor.*

109. Blackness carries negative connotations in English language and culture. Examples include: black code, black box, black Friday, black hand, black hole, black lung, black magic, black market, black Monday, black widow, blackmail, blackguard, black art, black ball, black bile, black book, blacklist, black death, black eye, blackout, black cat, and black lie. In *The Oxford English Dictionary* of 1600, blackness is defined as "stained with dirt, filthiness, baseness, ugliness, danger, evil, repulsion," and even as "sin." Blackness was associated with the devil, disaster, death, fear, ill-omen, and unpleasantness. The culture of the Elizabethan era linked blackness to savagery, evil, filth, misfortune, heathenism, impropriety, libidinous impulse, and bestial sexuality. English travelers erroneously wrote of Africans as people without God, laws, religion, language, or government. A negative imagery of blackness still exists today. In the United States, Blacks are portrayed as lazy, stupid, criminals, drug addicts, rapists, and murderers.

110. Thomas Jefferson was one of the authors of The Declaration of Independence. In its preamble he wrote, "We hold these truths to be self-evident, that all men are created equal, that they are endowed by their creator with certain inalienable rights that among these are Life, Liberty, and the pursuit of Happiness." The key words in this statement are *equality* and *liberty.* Apparently none of the founding

fathers believed in human equality. Later, in his Notes on Virginia, Jefferson wrote that Blacks were "dull, tasteless." He also praised the White race for their "flowing hair." Was his racial assessment a kind of ethnocentrism? Furthermore, in The Constitution of the United States, a Black person was considered three-fifths of a person. On his Monticello estate in Virginia, Jefferson owned hundreds of slaves whom he never manumitted. He did not stop Virginia from "slave breeding" and "bleeding." While Ambassador in Paris and throughout his presidency and retirement, rumors persisted that he was the father of Sally Hemings' (his Black slave-concubine) children. As Professor Charles Ogletree of Harvard University pointed out, "Thomas Jefferson was eloquent in his writings, but contradictory, inconsistent and hypocritical in his practice."

111. Intelligence Quotient (IQ) and Standard Achievement Tests (SAT) are used in United States schools as a means to not only evaluate student performance, but also to discriminate against minorities, particularly Blacks. The average combined SAT score is about 1150 out of 1600. Blacks are shown to score lower than any other racial grouping (an average of about 750 points). This is not due to inherent innate intellectual inferiority, but to socio-economic factors.

112. In heterogeneous societies, especially in the United States, the Caribbean Islands, and some borderline North African-Arab countries, color consciousness is accentuated. Lighter skin meant potential social acceptability and mobility. Mixed offspring were often ashamed of the residue of Africanity in their hair texture and shape of their noses. Some bleached their skin with chemicals, while others went as far as having their noses operated on to look Caucasian. In color conscious Haiti, mulattos were classified according to the shade of their color as sacatra, marabou, grimaud, and sang-mele. In the United States, until the late 1960s, Blacks were obsessed with the process of "passing" or "whitening out." The terms Black and African, which are presently used to identify the Black community in the United States, were considered negative and offensive. In the United States, employment categories in certain specific industries, admission in specific prestigious schools, housing patterns, and even religious aspirations reflect Social Darwinist philosophy. Color consciousness in traditional Africa was quite different from that of

the Europeans. Ancient Egyptians referred to the light-skinned contemptuously as the men of Arvad. In the Somali culture they still consider Whites as being infected with leprosy. In traditional and modern Burundi culture, Whites are referred to as *ibisigo* (ghosts). In Swahili culture, Whites are referred to as *baryane* (monkey-like). Blackness in African traditional culture was considered a color of beauty. In Burundi, traditional white clothes symbolized sadness and were worn during funeral ceremonies.

GLOSSARY

ABAGANWA. Chief or prince.

ABAHIMA. Ethnic Abatutsi subclan.

ABAHUTU. Ethnic group of Negroid stock (do not confuse with *abahutu* = serfs).

ABAMI. Kings

ABAPFUMU. Witch doctor.

ABARUNDI. People.

ABASHINGANTAHE. Wise men, judges.

ABASHITSI. Visitors (do not confuse with the callers of the dead).

ABATEREKAZI. Keepers of pythons. Guardians of Abami burial grounds.

ABATUTSI. Ethnic group of hamitic origin.

ABATWA. Ethnic group of Pygmoid classification.

ABATWARE. Sub-chiefs.

ABAVURATI. Rainmakers.

EJO. Yesterday or tomorrow.

GIHANGA. The founder of Burundi.

IMANA. God. (do not confuse with *imana* = good luck)

IMPUZAMUGAMBI. The literal meaning is "those who have one aim." The metaphoric meaning is "anti-Tutsi terrorist organization."

INKOTANYI. The literal meaning is "those who fight courageously" or "tough fighters." The term refers to the Rwandan Patriotic Front army.

INTERAHAMWE. The literal meaning is "those who attack together." The metaphoric meaning is "Hutu death squads."

KARYENDA. Male sacred royal drum.

KERA. Long time ago.

KIRANGA. An invisible spirit.

MUKAKARYENDA. Wife of Karyenda drum.

MULOPWE. King.

SHEBUJA. Lord.

SIMBA. Lion.

UBU. Now.

UBUHAKE. From the verb *guhaka*. A mutual contract between *shebuja* (patron) and *umugaragu* (servant/slave).

UBUHAKE. Individuals who enter into an agreement of servitude that is not legally binding.

UBUSHINGANTAHE. Wise men and judges.

UMUGANWA. Chief.

UMUTUTSI. An ethnic group of hamitic stock.

UMWAMI. King.

BIBLIOGRAPHY

Adriaenssen, J. B. *Histoire du Ruanda-Urundi*. Polyc., 1951.

Albert, Ethel. "Rhetoric, Logic and Poetics in Burundi Culture." *American Anthropologist*, LXVI, Part 2, December 1964.

Anjo, J. "L'Affaire Ngendandumwe." *Remarques Africaines*, No. 306, 25 January 1968.

Arendt, Hannah. *The Origins of Totalitarianism*. World Publishing, 1958.

Arnoux, Les Pères. *Blancs aux Sources du Nile*. Paris: Editions St. Paul, 1948.

Bahutu. *The Bahutu Manifesto*, 1959.

Barahinyura, S.J. *Le Général-Major Havyarimana*. Frankfurt am-Main: 1988.

Batururimi, Elias. "Le Parti du Roi Mwambutsa IV." *Remarques Africaines*, No. 247, 25 August 1965.

——. "Où va le pays?" *Remarques Africaines*, Vol. 7, No. 252, 1965.

Becker, Ernest. *Escape from Evil*. Free Press, 1975.

Bender, David. *Racism in America*. Greenhaven Press, 1991.

Bennet, Lerone. *The Shaping of Black America*. Penguin Books, 1975.

Bennett, Arlene. *Eugenics as a Vital Internationalized Racism*. International Publishers, 1977.

Bimazubute, Gilles. "Le 19 octobre et après." *Remarques Africaines*, 17 October 1965.

——. "Le coup d'état du 10 octobre 1965." *Remarques Africaines*, 3 November 1965.

——. "Le Gouvernement Royal de Mwami Mwambutsa IV." *Remarques Africaines*, No. 250, October 1965.

——. "Mon père est intelligent." *Remarques Africaines*, No. 269, 29 June 1966.

——. "Le prix du silence." *Remarques Africaines*, No. 259, 9 February 1966.

——. "Les relations diplomatiques entre le Burundi et la Chine." *Remarques Africaines*, Vol. 7, No. 236.

Bogle, Donald. *Toms, Coons, Mulatoes, Mammies, and Bucks.* Bantam Books, 1974.

Botte, Roger. "Quand l'essential n'est pas ce que l'on dit, mais ce que l'on sait." *Politique Africaine*, No. 12, December 1983.

Bourgeois, R. "Banyarwanda et Barundi." *RCB*, Vol. 3, 1957.

Boutros-Ghali, Boutros. *An Agenda for Peace.* United Nations, 1992.

Bowen, Michael. "No Samaritan: The USA and Burundi." *Africa Report*, No. 18, 1973.

——. *Passing By: The United States and Genocide in Burundi.* Carnegie Endowment for International Peace, 1972.

Boyayo, A. *Abrégé d'histoire du Burundi.* Bujumbura.

Braham, Randolph. *The Politics of Genocide.* Columbia University Press, 1980.

Bridgman, Jon. *The Revolt of the Herero.* University of California Press, 1981.

Brodie, Fawn. *Thomas Jefferson: An Intimate History.* New York, 1974.

Buhrer, J. *L'Afrique Orientale Allemande et la Guerre 1914–1918.* Paris: Fournier, 1923.

Burundi. "L'Affaire Ngendandumwe." *Remarques Africaines*, Vol. 8, No. 265, 4 May 1966.

——. "Les Assassins du Prince Rwagasore." *Remarques Congolaises et Africaines*, Vol. 4, No. 11-20.

——. "Burundi and Rwanda Joined in Death." *Economist*, 9 April 1994.

——. "Burundi at Close Range." *Africa Report*, 1965.

——. "Burundi: Un seul peuple." October 1988.

——. "La chasse aux Hutu." *Revue Française d'Etudes Politiques Africaines*, No. 81, September 1972.

——. "Conference Politique du Rwanda et du Burundi." *Courier d'Afrique*, No. 1, 11 January 1961.

——. "Coup Collapses." *Facts on File*, 2 December 1993.

——. "Le destin tragique de Ntare V." *Remarques Africaines*, No. 400, 10 July 1972.

——. "Developement rural et democratic; une dilemme." *Politique Africaine*, 11 September 1993.

——. "Un document comprometant." *Remarques Africaines*, No. 263, 6 April 1966.

——. "Les elections au Rwanda et au Burundi." *Présence Africaine*, No. 39, 1961.

——. "General Elections and After." *Africa Digest*, December 1961.

——. "Genocide ou massacre." *Jeune Afrique*, No. 596, 10 June 1972.

——. "Mwezi Gisabo." *Jeune Afrique*, 1977.

——. "Nouveaux temoignages sur le Burundi." *Remarques Africaines*, No. 430-31, November 1973.

——. "The Passing of Mwamiship." *Africa Report*, January 1967.

——. *Plan quinquennal de developement.* Bujumbura: 1964-1968.

——. "A Political Trial." *Bulletin of the International Commission of Jurists*, July 1963.

Bwakira, M. "Le calme peut-it signifier l'indifférence pour les Barundi?" *Remarques Congolaises*, Vol. 5, No. 17, 24 May 1963.

Came, Barry. "A Scene From Hell." *Maclean*, 25 April 1994.

Cart, H. *Conception des rapports politiques au Burundi.* Brussels: Centre de Recherche et d'Information Socio-Politiques.

Castermans, J. *Au Burundi.* Didier Hatier, 1990.

Chalk, Frank. *The History and Sociology of Genocide.* Yale University Press, 1990.

Charny, Israel. *Toward the Understanding and Prevention of Genocide.* Westview Press, 1984.

——. *How Can We Commit the Unthinkable?* Westview Press, 1982.

Chase-Dunn. *Global Formation: Structure of World Economy.* Oxford University Press, 1988.

Cheru, F. *The Silent Revolution in Africa.* London: 1989.

Chorover, Stephen. *From Genesis to Genocide*. MIT Press, 1979.

Chretien, J.P. "Le Burundi." *Documentation Francaise*, February 1968.

——. "Les dix commandements du Hutu." *Politique Africaine*, No. 42, 1991.

——. *Hutu et Tutsi au Rwanda et au Burundi*. Paris: La Découverte, 1985.

——. "Un Nazisme tropical." *Liberation*, 1994.

——. "Le Rwanda et la France." *Esprit*, 1993.

Christen, Hanne. *Refugees and Pioneers: History and Field Study of a Burundian Settlement in Tanzania*.

Churchill, Ward. "Genocide: Toward a Functional Definition." *Alternatives*, 1986.

Cimpaye, Joseph. *Résumé d'histoire du Burundi*. Bujumbura: Office de l'Information.

Clarke, Henrik. *Christopher Columbus*. 1992.

Clay, Jason. "Genocide in Our Time." *UTNE Reader*, November–December 1989.

Cohen, John. *Africa Adio: The Watutsi*. New York: Ballantine Books, November 1966.

Conniff, Michael. *Africans in the Americas*. St. Martin's Press, 1964.

Coppens, P. *Le Mandat Belge du Ruanda-Urundi*. Brussels: 1927.

Copper, Charles. *Black Biblical Studies*. Black Light Fellowship, 1993.

Coser, Lewis. "The Visibility of Evil." *Journal of Social Issues*, Vol. 25, No. 1, 1969.

Cutler, Lloyd. "The Right to Intervene." *Foreign Affairs*, 64.

D'Hertefelt, Marcel. *Les Anciens royaumes de la Zone Interlacustre Meridionale: Rwanda, Burundi, Buha, Tervuren*. Belgium: Musée Royale de l'Afrique Centrale, 1962.

——. *Myth and Political Acculturation in Rwanda*. Rhodes-Livingston Institute, 1960.

Dadrian, Vahakn. "A Typology of Genocide." *International Review of Modern Sociology*, Vol. 5, No. 2, 1975.

——. *Genocide as a Problem of National and International Law*. 1989.

Dellicour, F. "La conquette du Ruanda-Urundi." *Bulletin des Séances*, 1935.

Deng, T. *Conflict Resolution in Africa*. The Brookings Institution, 1992.

DesForges. *Rwanda Under Musinga (1896-1931)*.

Destexhe, A. *Rwanda and Genocide in the Twentieth Century*. New York University Press, 1995.

Du Bois, Victor. "To Die in Burundi." *American Universities Field Staff Reports*, Vol. 16, No. 4, September 1972.

Eckhardt, W. "Civilian Deaths in Wartime." *Bulletin of Peace Proposals 20*, No. 1, 1989.

Elliot, Gil. *Twentieth Century Book of the Dead*. Scribners & Sons, 1972.

Fein, Helen. "Genocide: A Sociological Perspective." *Current Sociology*, Vol. 38, No. 1, 1990.

———. *Genocide Watch*. Yale University Press, 1992.

Gahungu, Pièrre. "Où va le royaume du Burundi?" *Rémarques Africaines*, Vol. 7, No. 248, 8 September 1965.

Gakuba, L. *Rwanda 1931-1959*. La Pensée Universelle, 1991.

Gatwa, T. "Les autres Chrétiens Rwandais." *La présence protestante*, 1990.

Gault, William. "Some Remarks on Slaughter." *American Journal of Psychiatry*, Vol. 128, No. 4, 1971.

Ghislain, J. *La Féodalité au Burundi*. Brussels: ARSOM, 1970.

Gilbert, Martin. *The Macmillan Atlas of the Holocaust*. Macmillan, 1982.

Gilles, A. "L'Umuganuro ou la fête du sorgho en Urundi." *Bulletin Juridique indigene*, No. 11, 1945–1946.

Girkens, G. *Les Batutsi et les Bahutu*. Belgium: IRSNB, 1949.

Girukwishaka, E. *Le Néopaganisme au Burundi: Nanga Yivuza, que vous en emble?*

Goldenberg, S. "Crimes Against Humanity." *Western Ontario Law Review*, 1945–1970.

Gottlieb, G. *States Against Nations*. Council of Foreign Relations, 1993.

Greenland, Jeremy. "Ethnic Discrimination in Rwanda and Burundi." *A World Survey*, edited by Willem A. Veershoven, Vol. 4. The Hague: Martinus Nijhoff, 1976.

Gurr, Robert. "Victims of State." *International Review of Victimology*, 1989.

Guy, R. *L'histoire inhumaine: Massacres et génocides des origines à nos jours*. Paris: Armand Colin, 1992.

Hadjor, K. "Africa in an Era of Crisis." *Africa World Press*, 1990.

Hammer, Joshua. "Deeper in Abyss." *Newsweek*, 25 April 1994.

———. "Escape from Hell." *Newsweek*, 16 May 1994.

———. "The Killing Fields." *Newsweek*, 23 May 1994.

Hanley, G. *Warriors and Strangers*. Hamish Hamilton, 1971.

Harden, Blaine. "Money Lenders Horrified by the Burundi Killings." *The Washington Post*, September 1989.

Harding, Vincent. *Black Power and the American Christ*. Porter Sargent, 1968.

Harff, Barbara. *The Etiology of Genocide*. Greenwood Press, 1987.

Harroy, J.P. *Le Ruanda-Urundi: Ses resources naturelles, ses populations*. Brussels: 1966.

———. *Burundi 1952–1962*. Brussels: Hayez, 1987.

Haselden, Kyle. *The Racial Problem in Christian Perspective*. Harper & Row, 1959.

Havolkof, Soren. "Is God an American?" *Survival International*, Copenhagen: 1981.

Hebblethwaite, P. "Blood Thicker then Water." *National Catholic Reporter*, 3 June 1994.

Henry, William. "Beyond the Melting Pot." *Time*, 9 April 1990.

Heusch, Luc. *Rois nés d'un coeur de vache*. Gallimand, 1982.

———. *Le Rwanda et la civilisation interlacustre*. University Libre de Bruxelles, 1966.

Hienaux, Jean. "Cultures pre-historiques de l'âge des métaux au Ruanda-Urundi et au Kivu; in Académie Royale des Sciences Coloniales." *Bulletin des Séances*, Vol. 2, No. 6, 1956.

———. "Notes sur une ancienne population du Ruanda-Urundi; Les Renges." *Zaire*, Vol. 10, No. 4, 1956.

——. *Racial Properties of the Natives of Ruanda-Urundi.* Anthropos, 1955.

Hitler, Adolf. *Mein kampf.* Houghton Mifflin, 1971.

Horowitz, Irving. *Taking Lives: Genocide & State Power.* New Jersey: Transaction Books, 1982.

Jentgen, P. *Les frontières du Ruanda-Urundi et le régime internationale de Tutelle.* Brussels: 1957.

Jones, William. *Is God a White Racist?* Doubleday, 1973.

Kagabo, Liboire. *A propos des récents évenements de Ntega et Marangara: Une refflexion critique.* Bujumbura: 1988.

Kagame, Abbé. "Le code ésotérique de la dynastie du Rwanda." *Zaire*, Vol. 1, No. 4, 1947.

——. "Les Hamites du Rwanda et du Burundi: Sont-ils des Gallas?" *Académie Royale des Sciences Coloniales, Bulletin des Séances*, 1956.

——. *Histoire du Rwanda.* Leverville, Congo: 1958.

——. *Les Milices du Rwanda précolonial.* Brussels: Académie Royale des Sciences d'Outre-Mer, 1963.

——. "La notion de génération appliquée à la génealogie dynastique et à l'histoire du Rwanda dès X ième - XI ième siècles à nos jours." *Académie Royale des Sciences Coloniales, Tome IX, Nouvelles Séries*, Brussels: 1959.

——. *Inganji Kalinga.* Kabwayi: 1959.

——. *Les milices du Rwanda pre-colonial.* Brussels: 1963.

——. *Inganji, Karinga, Kabwayi.* 1943.

——. "La Royauté: Origine du Pouvoir du Mwami." *In Rapport du Gouvernement Belge*, Brussels: 1927.

Kalibwami, J. "Le catholicisme et la societé rwandaise." *Présence Africaine*, 1991.

Kamukama, D. *Rwanda Conflict: Its Roots and Regional Implications.* Kampala: Fountain Publications, 1993.

Kayemba, Henry. *A State of Blood: The Inside Story of Idi Amin.* Grosset & Dunlop, 1977.

Kayoya, Michel. *Sur les traces de mon père.* Bujumbura: 1968.

——. *Entre deux mondes.* Bujumbura: 1970.

Keupens, J. *Essai d'histoire du Burundi*. Bujumbura: Presses Lavigérie, 1957.

———. "Le Burundi ancien et moderne." *Esquisse Historique*, January 1965.

Kierkegaard, S. *Attack Upon Christianity*. Princeton University Press, 1946.

Kiraranganya, B. "Le vrai visage de l'UNEBA." *Remarques Africaines*, Vol. 9, No. 285, 9 March 1967.

———. *La verité sur le Burundi*. Sherbrooke, Quebec: Naam Publications, Collection Civilisations, 1977.

Kisyeti, Gerard. "Le Tribalisme au Burundi." *Remarques Africaines*, Vol. 10, No. 326, 20 December 1968.

Klein, Herbert. *African Slavery in Latin America*. Oxford University Press, 1980.

Krop, P. *Le génocide Franco-Africain*. Paris: 1991.

Kuper, Leo. *The Pity of It All: Polarization of Racial Ethnic Relations*. London: Duckworth, 1977.

———. *Genocide: Its Political Use*. Yale University Press, 1981.

———. *The Prevention of Genocide*. Yale University Press, 1985.

Léchat, M. *Le Burundi Politique*. Usumbura: Service d'Information du Ruanda-Urundi.

Lemarchand, Réné. "Political Instability in Africa, the Case of Rwanda and Burundi." *Civilisations*, 1966.

———. *Rwanda and Burundi*. New York: Praeger, 1970.

———. "The Social Change and Political Modernization in Burundi." *Journal of Modern African Studies*, October 1970.

———. "Selective Genocide in Burundi." *Minority Rights Group Report*, No. 20, 1974.

———. "The Military in Former Belgian Africa," in Kelleher, (ed). *Political Military Systems: Comparative Perspectives*. Beverly Hills: Sage Publications, 1974.

———. "Ethnic Genocide." *Issue 5*, Summer 1975.

———. "Burundi: The Killing Fields Revisited." *Issue 18*, No. 1, 1989.

———. "L'Ecole historique Burundo-Francaise." *Politique Africaine*, No. 37, March 1990.

————. "Revolutionary Phenomena in Stratified Societies" *Civilisations*, 1968.

Lemkin, R. "Genocide as a Crime Under International Law." *American Journal of International Law*, 1947.

Levasseur, G. "The Prevention of Genocide." *Journal of International Commission of Jurists*, 1967.

Lewis, Norman. *The Missionaries.* London: Arrow Books, 1988.

Lifton, Robert. *The Nazi Doctors: Medical Killing and the Psychology of Genocide.* Basic Books, 1986.

Lillich, Richard. *Humanitarian Intervention and the United Nations.* University of Virginia Press, 1973.

Linden, Ian. *Church and Revolution in Rwanda.* New York: Manchester University Press, 1977.

Lomax, Louis. *To Kill A Black Man.* Halloway House, 1987.

Lorch. Donatella. "Massacre of Tutsi at Nyarubuye" *New York Times*, 3 June 1994.

————. "Specter of Ethnic Hate." *New York Times*, 24 April 1994.

Louis, W. Roger. *Ruanda-Urundi, 1884–1919.* Clarendon Press, 1963.

Loupias, P. "Traditions et légendes des Batutsi sur la création du monde et leur étrablisssement au Rwanda." *Anthropos*, Vol. 3, No. 1, 1908.

Madirisha, J. "Une république inopportune." *Remarques Africaines*, Vol. 9, No. 290, 18 May 1967.

Malkki, Lisa. *Poverty and Exile: Transformation in Historical Consciousness among Hutu Refugees in Tanzania.* University of Chicago Press, 1992.

Manirakiza, Marc. *De la monarchie à la première république.* Brussels: 1993.

————. *De la révolution au régionalisme.* Brussels: 1993.

Maquet, Jacques. *The Premises of Inequality in Rwanda.* Oxford University Press, 1961.

————. *Le problème de la domination Tutsi.* Brussels: 1949.

Markus, Andrew. *Governing Savages.* Allen and Bacon, 1990.

Masland, Tom. "Corpses Everywhere." *Newsweek*, 18 April 1994.

Mcary, Walter. *The Black Presence in the Bible*. Black Light Fellowship, 1990.

———. *Black Bible Chronicles*. African-American Family Press, 1993.

Melady, Thomas. *Burundi: The Tragic Years*. Orbis Books, 1974.

Meltzer, Milton. *The Truth about the Ku Klux Klan*. Franklin Watts, 1982.

Meyer, H. *Die Barundi: Eine volkerkundliche studie Aus Deutsch-Ostafrika*. Leipzig: 1916.

Michaels, M. "Descent into Mayhem." *Time*, 18 April 1994.

Micombero, M. "Déclaration du President du Burundi." *Remarques Africaines*, No. 271, August 1966.

Mirerekano, Paul. *Mbwire Gito Canje (Gito C'Uwundi Cumvireho)*. Usumbura: 1959.

Mizell, Linda. *Racism*. Walker & Company, 1992.

Morris, Donald. *The Washing of the Spears*. Simon & Schuster, 1965.

Morris, R. *Passing By: The United States and Genocide in Burundi, 1972*. Carnegie Endowment for International Peace, 1973.

Mosley, William. "What Color Was Jesus?" *African American Images*, 1987.

Moulaert, Gabriel. "La conquête du Ruanda-Urundi." *Bulletin Séances*, 1935.

———. "Réponse à Monsieur Ndaje." *Remarques Africaines*, No. 271, 25 August 1966.

———. *La République du Burundi*. Paris: 1971.

Mumford, Lewis. "The Morals of Extermination." *Atlantic 204*, No. 4, 1959.

Murphy, Brian. "Bodies Flow Over Falls." *New York Times*, 17 May 1994.

Mworoha, Emile. "Le cour du Roi Mwezi Gisabo (1952–1908)." *Etudes d'histoire Africaine*, Bujumbura, Burundi.

———. *Histoire du Burundi des origines à la fin du XIX ième siecle*. Paris: 1987.

Nahimana, F. *Le Blanc est arrivé, Le Roi est parti*. Kigali: 1987.

Ndagijimana, F. *L'Afrique face à ses défits*. Geneva: 1990.

Ndayishingire, P. "L'Intronisation d'Umwami." *Collections et civilisations de l'Afrique Centrale*, 1977.

Ndizeye, Charles. "Déclaration du Prince Royal." *Rémarques Africaines*, No. 271, 25 August 1966.

Niqueaux, Jacques. "Rwanda et Burundi: les frères ennemis aux sources du Nil." *Revue Nouvelle*, Vol. 43, No. 5, May 1966.

Nkundabagenzi. *Rwanda Politique 1958–60*. Centre de Recherche et d'Information Socio-Politiques, 1961.

Nsanze, Térence. "L'Edification de la République du Burundi au Carefour de l'Afrique." *Remarques Africaines*, 1970.

Nyankanzi, Edward L. *Burundi: Socio-Historical Approach to Politics*. AAIC International, 1994.

———. "Partition of Burundi: A Response to Ambassador Melady." *New York Times*, 1988.

———. "United Nations: Fourth Decade." *Diplomatic Magazine*, 1976.

———. *Which Way Africa?* (Collected Essays) AAIC International, 1992.

———. "Why Not UPRONA?" *PADUNABU Newsletter*, 1988.

Nyberg, Richard. "Bloodletting Sweeps Rwanda." *Christianity Today*, 16 May 1994.

Nzeyimana, Laurent. "Burundi: aux nouveaux hommes, au nouveau régime, de nouvelles institutions." *Remarques Africaines*, Vol. 9, No. 283.

O'Ballence, E. *The Secret War in the Sudan 1955–1972*. Archon Books, 1977.

O'Brian, C. "Biafra: Genocide & Discretion." *The Listner*, January 1969.

Omer, M. *Pleure ô Rwanda bien-aimé*. Vaillance-Ardenne, 1994.

Pages, A. *Un royaume hamite au centre de l'Afrique*. Brussels: 1933.

Painton, Priscilla. "Genocide Mumbo Jumbo." *Time*, 1990.

Pascoe, Elaine. *Racial Prejudice*. Franklin Watts, 1985.

Peraudin, J. *Naissance d'une église: Histoire du Burundi Chretien*. Bujumbura: Presses Lavigerie, 1963.

Peterson, S. "A Small Girl's Silence Tells Story of Burundi Crisis." *Christian Science Monitor*, 5 November 1993.

Piervis, Andrew. "Welcome to Ground Zero." *Time*, 20 June 1994.

Poincaré, N. "Rwanda." *Les éditions de l'Atelier*, 1995.

Porter, Jack. *Genocide and Human Rights: A Global Anthology.* University Press of America, 1982.

Press, Robert. "We Didn't Mean to Do It." *Economist*, 1993.

———. "Burundi Army Learns Democracy Has Roots." *Christian Science Monitor*, 29 October 1993.

———. "Military Coup in Burundi Dissolves New Democracy." *Christian Science Monitor*, 22 October 1993.

Pritchard, B. "Rwanda Terrorism: Tutsi Main Targets." *National Catholic Reporter*, June 1994.

Prunier, G. "Element pour une histoire de Front Patriotique Rwandais." *Politique Africaine*, No. 51, 1993.

———. *L'Ouganda et le Front Patriotique Rwandais*. Lille, 1992.

———. *The Rwanda Crisis: History of a Genocide*. Columbia University Press, 1995.

Ransdell, Eric. "Why is Rwanda Killing Itself?" *U. S. News & World Report*, 23 May 1994.

Rawson, David. "The Role of the United Nations in the Development of Ruanda-Urundi." An unpublished dissertation, American University, 1966.

Reuss, Conrad. "Réflexions sur l'aide de la Belgique au Burundi." *Etudes Congolaises*, Vol. 12, No. 2, April–June 1969.

Reynjens, Filip. *L'Afrique des grands lacs en crise, Rwanda, Burundi: 1988-1994*. Paris: Karthala, 1993.

———. "Burundi: 1972–1988: Continuite et changement." *Les cahiers du CEDAF*, No. 5, November 1989.

———. "Du bon usage de la science. L'école historique Burundo-Francaise." *Politique Africaine*, No. 37, March 1990.

Ridgeway, J. *Blood in the Face*. Thunder's Mouth, 1990.

Rodegem, F. "Burundi: La face cachée de la rébellion." *Intermediaire*, Vol. 4, June 1973.

Ruanda-Urundi. *Geography and History*. Brussels: Office of Public Information, 1956.

Rudipresse. *Bulletin hebdomadaire d'information, Usumbura (1957–1962)*.

Rugomana. *Les Rois du pays "Rundi" et les hommes qui y sont venue les premiers*. Zaire: 1957.

Rwanda. "The Underlying Causes." *Africa Report*, IX, No. 1, 1964.

Ryckmans, P. *Notes sur les titres et fonctions de la famille royale du Burundi*. Derscheid Collection, 1919.

——. *Une page d'histoire coloniale: L'Occupation Allemande dans l'Urundi*. Brussels: IRCB, 1953.

——. *La politique coloniale*. Brussels: Editions Germinal, 1958.

Sabimbona, S. "Une république révolutionaire." *Remarques Africaines*, Vol. 9, No. 285, 9 March 1967.

Samatar, Ahmed. *The Somali Challenge*. Lynne Riener Publishers.

Sasserath, Jules. *Le Ruanda-Urundi: Etrange royaume féodal*. Brussels: Editions Germinal, 1958.

Schmidt, R. *Abatare et Bezi*. Usumbura: 1953.

Schmidt, W. "Rwanda Puzzle: Is Uganda Taking Sides?" *New York Times*, 18 April 1994.

Schumacher, A. *Au Rwanda: Considérations sur la nature de l'homme*. Brussels: 1949.

Sebasoni, S. *Condition humaine et tradition Rwandaise*. Brussels.

Segal, Aaron. "The Massacre in Rwanda." *Fabian Research Series*, 11 April 1964.

Sharlet, Jeff. "Burundi Bleeds." *Nation*, 17 January 1994.

Shibura, Albert. *Burundi: Temoignages*. Bujumbura: 1993.

Shoumatoff, A. "Flight from Death." *New Yorker*, 20 June 1994.

——. "Rwanda's Aristocratic Guerrillas." *New York Times Magazine*, 13 December 1994.

Simons, S. "Coutumes et institutions des Barundi." *Editions de la révue juridique*, 1944.

Smyth, Frank. "Blood Money and Geopolitics." *Nation*, 2 May 1994.

——. "French Guns, Rwandan Blood." *New York Times*, 14 April 1994.

———. "Arming Rwanda: The Arms Trade and Human Rights Abuses in the Rwandan War." *A Report by Human Rights Watch*, January 1994.

Snowdon, F. *Blacks in Antiquity*. Harvard University Press, 1970.

Soulik, S. "Interview du Colonel Michel Micombero." *Remarques Africaines*, No. 305, 11 January 1968.

Staub, Ervin. *Roots of Evil*. Cambridge University Press, 1989.

Stearns, S. "An Uneasy Peace." *Africa Report*, January/February 1994.

———. "Refugees Continue to Flee as the UN Condemns Coup." *Christian Science Monitor*, 27 October 1993.

Sterling, Claire. "Chou-en-lai and the Watutsi." *Reporter*, 14 March 1964.

Stocker, H. *German Imperialism in Africa*. London: 1986.

Todorov, T. *The Conquest of America: The Question of the Other*. Harper & Row, 1984

Trimingham, S. *The Influence of Islam Upon Africa*. Praeger, 1968.

Trouwborst, A. "L'Accord de clientèle et l'organisation politique au Burundi."*Anthropologica*, Vol. 4, No. 1, 1962.

Uganda.*Uganda & Human Rights*. Geneva: International Commission of Jurists, 1977.

Ugeux, E. "Une interview exclusive de Mwami Mwambutsa IV, ancien roi du Burundi." *Rémarques Africaines*, No. 403, 10 July 1972.

———. "Après sept ans de la république, le bilan d'une tragédie." *Remarques Africaines*, No. 429, October 1973.

Vaiter, M. *Je n'ai pas pu les sauver tous*. Plon, 1995.

Van der Burgt, J. *Un grand peuple de l'Afrique équatoriale*. Bois-le-Duc, 1903.

Van Sertima, I. *They Came Before Columbus: The African Presence in Ancient America*. Random House, 1976.

Vansina, Jan. "Notes sur l'histoire du Burundi." *Aequatoria*, Vol. 14, 1961.

———. *L'Evolution du royaume Rwanda des origines à 1900*. Brussels: Académie Royale des Sciences d'Oûtre-Mer, 1962.

———. *La légende du passé*. Tervuren, 1972.

Vidal, C. "Le Rwanda des anthropologues et le fétichisme de la vâche." *Cahiers d'etudes Africaines*, Vol. 9, No. 3, 1969.

——. "Rwanda, Burundi: La politique de haine." *Les Temps Modernes*, No. 583, 1995.

—— *Sociologie des passions*. Paris: 1991.

Vincent, Marc. *L' Enfant au Ruanda-Urundi*. Brussels: IRCB, 1954.

Von Clausewitz. *Vom Krieg*. Dummlin Verlag, 1966.

Watson, Catherine. "The Death of Democracy." *Africa Report*, 1994.

Webster, John. *Political Development of Rwanda and Burundi*. New York: Maxwell Graduate School of Citizenship and Public Affairs, Syracuse University, 1966.

Weeks, George. "The Armies of Africa." *Africa Report*, IX, No. 1, 1964.

Weinstein, Warren. "The Limits of Military Dependency: The Case of Belgian Aid to Burundi 1961–1973." *Journal of African Studies*, 1976.

——. *Historical Dictionary of Burundi*. Metuchen, New Jersey: Scarecrow Press, 1976.

——. *Political Conflicts and Ethnic Strategies: The Burundi Case*. Syracuse University Program of Eastern African Studies, 1976.

Weisberg, H. *The Congo Crisis 1964*. 1972.

Weiss, S. *Wahima, Watusi, and Wajambo in Deutsch Ostafrika*. Munich: Lehmann, 1926.

Wharton, Clifton. "Democracy's Bleeding." *New York Times*, 9 April 1994.

White, Walter. *Rope and Faggot*. Arno Press, 1968.

William, Isidor. *Genocide and Modern Age*. Greenwood Press, 1987.

Wilmore, G. "The Black Messiah." *Journal of Interdenominational Theological Center*, Vol. 2, 1974.

Wolbers, Marian. *Burundi*. Chelsea House Publishers, 1989.

Wood, David."The Armed Forces of African States (see Burundi)." *Adelphi Papers*, No. 27, April 1966.

Wooding, Dan. *Uganda Holocaust*. Grand Rapids, Michigan: Zondervan, 1980.

Zangrie, L. "Quelques traces éthnologiques de l'origine Egyptienne des Batutsi." *Jeune Afrique*, No. 15, 1951.

Zartman, W. *Destiny of a Dynasty*. Columbia, South Carolina: Brian, 1964.

Zuure, B. *L'Ame du Murundi*. Beauchesne, 1932.

———. *Souvenirs de mon sejour au Burundi*. Vulpenkrassen, 1930.

INDEX

ALSO OF INTEREST FROM SCHENKMAN BOOKS

BLACK INTELLECTUALS AND THE DILEMMA
OF RACE AND CLASS IN TRINIDAD
Oxaal, Ivar
334 pp., 1982
Paper $22.95 (0-87073-417-2)
A perceptive description of the events leading to independence in the multiracial setting of Trinidad. Covers the rise of Creole nationalism, the role of intellectuals in Trinidad, and offers a social study of both Trinidad and Tobago in the aftermath of independence.

THE BLACK WOMAN CROSS-CULTURALLY
Steady, Filomina, editor
640 pp., 1985
Paper $24.95 (0-87073-346-X)
An outstanding volume that brings together a body of relevant but previously fragmented and scattered literature on the black woman via a cross-cultural perspective. Discusses the lives of women in Africa, the United States, South America, and the Caribbean.

INTERNATIONAL RELATIONS OF THE MIDDLE EAST
AND NORTH AFRICA
Al-Marayati, Abid A., editor
540 pp., 1984
Cloth $29.95 (0-87073-824-0)
An interdisciplinary approach to the factors affecting policy decisions in Middle Eastern and North African nations. Studies the role of outside powers on the framing of domestic and foreign policies, and the ways in which inter-Arab conflicts influences each of these nations.